THE ARROW AND THE SWORD

by the same author

HISTORY
    King James I
    George Villiers, First Duke of Buckingham
    John Hampden
    Charles and Cromwell

FICTION
    Captain Thomas Schofield

PLAYS
    Rose and Glove
    The Seven Deadly Virtues
    In a Glass Darkly
    Various Heavens
    Mr. Gladstone
    Queen Elizabeth
    The Death of Don Juan

RELIGION
    Paul a Bondslave
    (A Radio Play on St. Paul)
    The Story Without an End
    (Dramatized Meditations on the Life of Christ)
    Were You There . . . ?
    (Meditations for Holy Week)

THE ARROW
AND THE SWORD

An Essay in Detection

*being an enquiry into the nature of the
deaths of William Rufus and Thomas
Becket, with some reflections on the
nature of medieval heresy*

by

HUGH ROSS WILLIAMSON

with a preface by
The Reverend V. A. Demant, D.Litt.
Canon of St. Paul's

FABER AND FABER LTD
24 Russell Square
London

First published in Mcmxlvii
by Faber and Faber Limited
24 Russell Square London W.C.1
Printed in Great Britain by
Latimer Trend & Co Ltd Plymouth
All rights reserved

To

PATRICK

Who asked the Question

CONTENTS

PREFACE BY DR. V. A. DEMANT   *page* xi

AUTHOR'S FOREWORD   1

PART I: THE UNDERLYING BELIEFS

I. THE PROBLEM AND THE BACKGROUND   7
   (1) The Question   7
   (2) The Pre-Christian Empires   9
   (3) The Stream of Heresy   11

II. THE CULTURE PATTERN AND THE CULT   19
   (1) The Blood Sacrifice   19
   (2) The Human Victim   21
   (3) The Pattern and the Myths   23
   (4) The Mysteries   25

III. THE METAMORPHOSES OF MITHRA   28
   (1) Persia and Babylon   28
   (2) The Host of Heaven   31
   (3) The Stoics   36
   (4) The Logos   38
   (5) The Gnostics   41
   (6) The Manichees   46
   (7) The Albigenses, or Cathars   48
   (8) Mithra in Britain   52

IV. JEHOVAH AND JESUS   58
   (1) Palestine   58
   (2) The One God   59
   (3) Gerizim   62
   (4) Jerusalem renounces the Sun   64
   (5) The Figure of Wisdom   66
   (6) The Fulfilment of the Gentiles   70
   (7) The Spirit   74

V. THE NATURE OF LOVE   76
   (1) Platonic Love   76
   (2) The Conspiracy of Silence   79
   (3) Clues in History   82

CONTENTS

PART II: THE HISTORICAL CIRCUMSTANCES

VI. THE ELEVENTH CENTURY BACKGROUND   *page* 91

    (1) The Witches   91
    (2) A Dance   96
    (3) The Devil   101
    (4) Rufus and Becket   105

VII. WILLIAM RUFUS   108

    (1) The Red King   108
    (2) His Name   109
    (3) His Oath   111
    (4) His Associates   113
    (5) His Character   115
    (6) His Death   117

VIII. THOMAS BECKET   120

    (1) The Angevins   120
    (2) Thomas of London   122
    (3) Henry and Becket in 1170   126
    (4) The Murder in the Cathedral   128
    (5) The Omissions of John of Salisbury   130
    (6) Echoes of the Cult   133

PART III: THE THEOLOGICAL IMPLICATIONS

IX. THE HERESY   *page* 139

    (1) The Puritanism of 'The Pure'   139
    (2) The Cathar Trinity   143
    (3) The Consolamentum   146
    (4) The Four 'Sacraments'   147
    (5) The Endura   150

X. THE REPLY OF ORTHODOXY   152

    (1) Doctrinal Definition   152
    (2) Practical Reactions   155
    (3) The Joachists   157

XI. THE NATURE OF THE CHURCH   159

    (1) The Church and the World   159
    (2) Sacramentalism   164
    (3) Christianity a Mystery Religion   167

XII. AGAPE AND EROS: A Note   170

INDEX   179

PREFACE

by The Reverend V. A. Demant, D.Litt.
Canon of St. Paul's

This book of Mr. Hugh Ross Williamson's seems to me to be important for three reasons. It includes a piece of historic detection which claims to overturn the accepted account of the way William Rufus and Thomas Becket met their deaths; it provides a conspectus of the very powerful 'Cathar' movement which, though of pre-Christian origin penetrated deeply into the bosom of Christendom itself; it opens up a necessary discussion of the relation between the Church's 'orthodoxy' and 'heresy', in this case a very special and formidable kind of heresy at that.

I am glad to use this preface for stating what I think the significance of these considerations to be, all three of which in some way concern fundamental interpretations of human existence. The author knows this and he is the first to admit that in this essay he has only stated a case and raised issues which are beyond the scope of a single volume and the power of one man's mind to dispose of conclusively.

Mr. Ross Williamson is already well known as a writer of some provocativeness on historical subjects. He has lately shown gifts for presenting through broadcasting the central drama of the Christian Faith. And as a parish priest in the ministry of the Church of England he is known to a smaller but grateful body of people as a much valued pastor and teacher. In this book he now comes forward as a religious thinker, one concerned with movements of spiritual vitality rather than with theology or philosophic systems in themselves; but the point which this essay leads up to is the theological and philosophical issues raised for the historic Church by one of its most seductive rivals. So while the subject matter of the book is one of the great heresies, the author's lively interest and competence in it are directed precisely to the extent to which its understanding may minister to the confirmation and strengthening of the main orthodox position of historic Christianity.

I now indicate what seems to me the significance of the three tasks this work undertakes. First of all the whole treatment is given a piquant and concrete turn by including in its central portion an unusual account of two prominent figures in English history. The interpretation of the deaths of William the Second of England and of Thomas Becket as ritual deaths plays only a secondary and illustrative part in the book, and many readers may find it, as I do, not conclusively established so far as the evidence here presented goes. But Mr. Ross Williamson makes out a *prima facie* case and some odd things certainly fit together on this view. He acknowledges that the idea was suggested by others; his part has been to show that it is congruous with the extent to which the cult of 'the Cathari' was a dominant and popular force in the Middle Ages and had invaded the life of Church and State. The notion that two such highly placed persons as a King and an Archbishop should have been members of a heretical movement, and one with such pagan affiliations, will certainly come as a jolt to many readers. Some of them will probably dislike the idea for the general reason that its concealment until now implies a very successful conspiracy in the past to hide the facts. If this thesis is true, they will feel, then both we and our historians have been very effectively hoaxed— and English people in particular are perhaps inclined to resent the supposition that they could be the victims of a highly skilled plan to put them off the scent. There have been, in my opinion, several such successful conspiracies in history and literature. We should not rule them out of court because to admit them as successful means to acknowledge that we have been misled by a sustained and astute co-operative effort in planned intelligence.

I am labouring this point that we moderns and especially modern Englishman should not impatiently brush aside a somewhat esoteric account of historic incidents out of the pride which will not admit that men in the past have made us believe for a long time what they wanted us to believe. I am not finally convinced that these two deaths were ritual self-immolations, and the author allows that his case is not so strong in the case of Becket as in that of Rufus. But with the latter Mr. Ross Williamson has an easier task in that the circumstances of Rufus's death are much more a matter of dark ignorance than in that of Becket. For the Murder in the Cathedral there is an accepted account, in spite of some discrepancies, which has to be a good deal 'interpreted and corrected' in order to support the thesis here presented. The Arrow-shot in the New Forest is all the history books give us about the end of William the Second. It is therefore easier to use an unusual explanation in this case than in the other, for there is no accepted tradition of the how and the why of the event which the new interpretation has to wrestle with.

Then, apart from this question of historical authenticity, quite a number of susceptibilities will be painfully aroused by the suggestion of Thomas Becket's participation in a movement which so frequently became at issue with the Church and which in William Rufus's case was part and parcel of his anti-clericalism. Thomas of Canterbury has become so much a symbol of the Church's resistance to secular intrusion into her institutions and life. But now that we have also an interpretation of Dante as a member of the Order of Knights-Templar, with similar gnostic, dualistic and esoteric trends, written by a Roman Catholic priest-scholar, this kind of touchiness will have to be overcome. And if further knowledge should establish that Becket was an initiate it will be of importance and interest to know whether there was any marked change in his relation to the cult when he ceased to be Chancellor and became Archbishop.

The second and chief value of Mr. Ross Williamson's book is that it strings on one thread a number of tendencies often of diverse historic roots but of a cognate religious temper which is clearly identifiable. At the period in which he is most interested the representatives of this movement can be conveniently called the 'Cathari'. One phase of the movement, that of the Albigenses, is perhaps the best known to historians. But the importance of the sketch given in this work springs from its showing the 'Cathar' cults as one representative of a very deep rooted and recurring religious force. To mention only its roots in Mithraism, its links with the gnostics, its theological dualism, its asceticism, the rituals of life and death as cosmic mysteries, the appeal of the troubadours, Arthurian legends and the cult of the Holy Grail, the passions aroused for and against witchcraft, the intimate connection between sex and religion—all these things are sufficient testimony to the deep rooted vitality of a stream of religious consciousness which cannot be superciliously dismissed by rationalists and moralists. I am inclined to think that if the historic church does not take hold of the modern soul at the same deep level, it is this kind of heresy that will be revived to fill the gap between an eviscerated, over-cerebrated and pelagian Christianity of the West and the secular idolatries which are its immediate supplanters. Already there are forces harking back to some form of Gnosticism as a more robust religiousness than orthodoxy often seems now to present.

The appeal and force of the whole cluster of beliefs and practices which Mr. Ross Williamson describes as 'the Heresy' lie partly in the ease with which men turn to gnostic and dualistic doctrines away from the more hardly held tensions in orthodox Christianity. I shall comment on this point a little later on. But apart from the interpretations of existence involved, 'the Heresy' exercises a seductive pull for less intellectual reasons. For one thing it faces squarely the force of evil in the world as a positive thing which it is too readily assumed can be overcome by morals or politics or the march of progress or the right institutions. It offers instead a way of deliverance or 'catharsis' which touches the deepest psychic springs of human life. However misplaced the source of evil may be by its devotees, either by setting the Evil Power on an equality with the good God or by making the phenomenal world the seat of evil, 'the Heresy' has set the 'powers of darkness' in sufficiently high places to give the moral struggle a titanic and cosmic inspiration. In this way it tended to call out energies and commitments when the more psychological and voluntaristic cast of the Western mind became wearisome. Then again 'the Heresy' had the recurring appeal of a mystery cult, and Mr. Ross Williamson brings out the necessary point that Christian orthodoxy is in its own authentic way a cult of initiates and should not shy away from living as such because it can falsely be assimilated to the pagan mysteries. Further, 'the Heresy' had all the advantages of a movement in which the rituals forming the souls of its devotees were often protesting counterparts of the more regular and sober rituals of the Church. It had the appeal which all more exciting and heretical enterprises have over the well established. Above all 'the Heresy' used to the full the hold which an apocalyptic proclamation for 'the present age' can always exercise. And when it takes the form of the pretension that 'now' the final revelation of the divine purpose for the world is to be unfolded, as in the teaching of Joachim of Flora that the age of the Spirit is inaugurated, the pull is very great indeed upon religiously intense personalities who have not learnt to receive the grace of God in the delays of His Kingdom.

Mr. Ross Williamson gives us a great deal of information to show how strongly these appeals operated. He also calls attention to what might look to us rather like a paradox, namely that the movement was both Puritan and popular.

There are two things to be said about that. In the first place the asceticism of the movement, its championing of platonic or uranian love and its attribution of earthly sexual love to a fallen and sinful condition, has little in common with what we know of Puritanism from the later Protestant sects. And in the second place, the popularity of such a common life-denying asceticism, such as Mr. Ross Williamson finds in the people's devotion to Rufus and Becket, is quite likely the demand of a populace for the vicarious asceticism of an *élite*. Just as modern Christians often champion the cause of missions or become vocal about race discrimination elsewhere, out of a feeling that someone must be Christian for us, so it seems that men and women in the Middle Ages were only too glad that a good few gentry and some eminent persons were being ascetic and spiritual in their place.

The third matter of importance raised by this book is the whole relation of the historic Church to such heretical movements as that of the 'Cathari'. On this theme I wish Mr. Ross Williamson could have made his treatment fuller. But he has made the significant point quite clear. It is that no Christian Church could come to terms with a religious movement of this kind, or even regard it merely as a slight aberration from the Church's central affirmations. It was in fact a rival religion and almost succeeded in being a counter-Church with its own rival and ritual system. The historic Church which had assumed the role of spiritual guide to a world in its day-to-day life and problems, could not but condemn a sect which repudiated marriage, ignored the rights of property, set loose to the ties of society and civil order, regarded matter as the seat of evil. But of deeper significance is the clear incompatibility between the theology of the 'Cathari' and that of Biblical and Catholic Christianity. Mr. Ross Williamson brings out that any form of gnostic dualism is a pre-Christian religion which the Biblical revelation was specifically given in order to overcome. The resurgence of this pagan religiousness always presents the Church with the same kind of chal-

lenge to its central positions as it had to deal with, for instance, in its struggle with Arianism. In fact the Cathar
theology had some close similarities with the Arian doctrine,
especially in regarding Christ as a creature, but neither incarnate nor ascended. And the crucial issue between Christianity and all attempts to insinuate a pre-Christian religion
by using the camouflage of Christian terminology lies in the
mutual exclusiveness of the Biblical doctrine of Creation
and all forms of dualism. Pre-Christian pagan religion whenever it expressed itself in philosophy or theology, either had
to posit two opposed divinities, one good one bad, like the
Ormuzd and Arihman of Zoroastrianism or they drew a line
through divinity between the ultimate source of all things
and the working gods who controlled the world. All these
religions make a valiant attempt to account by knowledge
(gnosis) for the chasm between the One out of whom all
things come and the concrete cluster of particular creatures
that make up the world, and a world largely of discord and
evil at that. To divide the godhead into two was a simpler
thing—simpler to the intellect that dispenses with faith—
than to accept the Judaic-Christian dogma of the one God
who created the world and saw that it was good, the *I am who
am* of Exodus, the Lord of History as well as the direct up-
holder of and knower of each single hair of one's head. And
it was simpler too for the intellect and for action to point
two levels of the god-head when the existence of evil had to
be faced. The business god who created the world and deals
with human affairs becomes in a way a lapsed deity. So in the
Cathar pantheon 'Jehovah' is equated with the Demiurge.
The good God dwells in light inaccessible, except to *the
Illuminati*. I therefore think that Harnack's dictum which
Mr. Ross Williamson quotes is the reverse of the truth.
Harnack said that orthodoxy and the paganism that so
easily put on a Christian dress had the same theology but
different mythologies. It is quite clear that where gnostic
and dualistic heresies succeeded in invading the Christian

universe of discourse, it was rather the case of a different and
alien religion adopting the Christian Mythology. Mr. Ross
Williamson's thesis does support this interpretation though
he has not consciously presented it in that way.

In my brief comments on the force of the Cathar movement I suggested that some of that force was due to the appeal
of a religion which had a definitely cosmic context and this
would naturally exercise an attraction within the orbit of Western Christendom, where Christianity tended to be presented
very much in purely ethical and psychological terms. And it had
also the appeal which gnosis and initiation and access to secret
springs of spiritual energy always have for groups of people
who feel the need of power for personal and social ends.

The 'Cathari' presented the Church then with a much
deeper problem than that of a vital, energetic and apocalyptic
spirituality struggling against the heavy weight of a conventional and 'established' Church religion. It is the perennial
burden of the Church to cope with the movements that often
justly make that criticism of her, but use the justice of the
complaint to smuggle in an intolerable rival religion.

In a book that raises so many issues of historic tendencies
and of judgment on their significance, of theological or
philosophical importance, of competing ways of life and cult,
there are bound to be some mistakes. But I believe that by
bringing out such questions as are involved in this thesis,
the author has performed a valuable service. As an ecclesias-
tic I am naturally most interested in the consequences for
the strengthening of the influence of the historic Christian
Church. In coping with a number of 'heresies' which are,
as it were, heresies from within, the Church has sharpened
and defined its own teaching and has sometimes deepened it.
But in the case of this kind of heresy—definitely a heresy
from without—that particular benefit has not yet been
worked out. Mr. Ross Williamson's book makes a real contribution to the possibility of that task being undertaken
and carried through.

FOREWORD

The genesis of this essay explains the purpose of it. In a novel about the seventeenth century I had invented the character of a witch who knew 'something of the secret of such deaths as those of William Rufus and Thomas Becket'. A friend, having read the book, asked me what this meant. When I explained that it was the—to me, conventional—theory that these deaths were the ritual killing of the Divine King in the witch-cult, he said in amazement: 'But surely you don't believe that blithering nonsense!' I said I thought that, on the whole, I did. He asked why. I said that it was very difficult to explain shortly. He said that he presumed it was impossible to explain at all and that that was my way of getting out of it. I said that, if he really wanted to know, I would attempt to put it on paper for him as shortly as I could.

The result of this was roughly the substance of Parts I and II of the present work. These are exactly what they purport to be—an essay in detection with a limited and specific objective. They are not a study of anthropology, theology, eroticism or comparative religion—though all these are involved in it—and if these weightier matters may seem at the outset to overshadow the simple historical point, it is because without some understanding of them that point cannot even be seen.

Nor is *The Arrow and the Sword* a work of scholarship, in the technical sense. The various quotations and references are to be taken, not as an advertisement of the range of my reading, but as evidence of my reluctance to advance my own

1

unsupported opinions in fields in which I cannot claim original
research among manuscripts. Even the thesis is not new—
though I think I have advanced for the first time certain arguments in its favour—and the conclusion is necessarily inconclusive. I have not so much tried to prove a case as to select
and co-ordinate certain evidence which may suggest that there
is a case to be proved.

I wrote the original essay at St. Deiniol's Library, Hawar-
den, during the last six months of 1942, but on the advice of
friends who read it in manuscript refrained from publishing
it in that form. It was felt that, in print, it might find its way
into hands for which it was not intended, and disturb un-
necessarily the faith of the simple.

Three years later, however, in 1945, it seemed to me on re-
reading the manuscript that there was a certain general interest in the thesis and, through the kindness of Mr. T. S. Eliot,
it was submitted to Canon V. A. Demant. He advised me to
supplement the essay with a third part, in which the theological implications of the earlier parts should be more fully
explored. This I have now done, but I am more conscious
than ever that, even with this addition, the book remains nothing more than an essay, touching only the fringe of the subject and valuable, if at all, only as a stimulus to profounder
thinkers and better scholars.

Also I think that *The Arrow and the Sword* even in its present form still requires the *caveat* with which I prefaced the
original essay—that it is not written for and should not be
read by children or those of the mental age of children. Possibly it had better be left alone, too, by those who cannot
understand the meaning of the Catholic Faith as suggested
by the two following quotations.

'Catholics acknowledge', writes Karl Adam in *The Spirit
of Catholicism*, 'without any shame, nay with pride, that
Catholicism cannot be identified simply and wholly with
primitive Christianity, nor even with the Gospel of Christ, in
the same way that the great oak cannot be identified with the

2

tiny acorn. There is no mechanical identity, but an organic
identity. And we go further and say that thousands of years
hence Catholicism will probably be even richer, more luxuriant, more manifold in dogma, morals, law and worship than
the Catholicism of the present day. A religious historian of
the fifth millennium A.D. will without difficulty discover in
Catholicism conceptions and forms and practices which derive from India, China and Japan. . . . The Gospel of Christ
would have been no living Gospel, and the seed which He
scattered no living seed, if it had remained for ever the tiny
seed of A.D. 33, and had not struck root, and had not assimilated foreign matter and had not by the help of this foreign
matter grown up into a tree, so that the birds of the air dwell
in its branches.'

And Father Tyrell, writing in 1898 in an essay which received the *imprimatur*, says: 'The militant Protestant delights
to dwell on the analogies between Romanism and Paganism;
we too may dwell on them with delight, as evidence of that
substantial unity of the human mind which underlies all surface diversities of mode and language, and binds together, as
children of one family, all who believe in God the Rewarder
of them that seek Him, who is no respecter of persons. What
man in his darkness and sinfulness has feebly been trying to
utter in every nation from the beginning, that God has formulated and written down for him in the great Catholic religion
of the Word made Flesh.'

The Catholic, who accepts Revelation, is free to explore
the matters of which I have written in safety from hurt or
heresy. From the analogy between a primitive procession and
dance of those who have partaken of the body and blood of
their god, the Bull, and a modern Corpus Christi festival, the
Catholic and the Rationalist draw opposite conclusions. The
Rationalist considers that the primitive rite discredits the
Christian truth; the Catholic knows that it reinforces it. Rationalist publishers have indeed rendered a very great service
to the Church by making accessible to the public in cheap

3

FOREWORD

and popular form many of the discoveries of anthropology which so greatly strengthen the faith of the Faithful.

Though this book is occupied with examining heresy, it contains, to the best of my knowledge and belief, nothing heretical in its conclusions; and should anything be so phrased as to give scandal to the instructed, I should wish to emend it in a subsequent edition.

I also wish to thank many friends who have criticized the thesis and, in particular, while in no way involving them in the views expressed, Canon V. A. Demant, Mr. T. S. Eliot, Mr. Herbert Read and the Rev. Alec Vidler.

HUGH ROSS WILLIAMSON

London.
Feast of the Assumption of
the Blessed Virgin Mary.
1946.

I

THE UNDERLYING
BELIEFS

Chapter I

THE PROBLEM AND THE BACKGROUND

---

1. *The Question*

'There is a strong body of evidence', writes Dr. Margaret Murray in *The God of the Witches*, 'to show that in the primitive cult of Western Europe the god was sacrificed. The Christian inquisitors are unanimous on this point and the direct accounts given at the trials of the witches confirm their statements.' She adds the necessary *caveat* that any investigation of the subject requires the shedding of preconceived notions or modern ideas read backward into the past. In this particular case, even the contemporary accounts, as they are written by the irreconcilable enemies of the cult, are biased, and, in many particulars, ill-informed or ignorant of the real nature of the matters with which they are dealing. But the assertion that the sacrifice was offered in this country within the period of its written history rests upon evidence which would be admitted were it adduced in the case of an African tribe or an Oriental religion.

Two such 'Divine Victims' of the witch-cult were, probably, William II, King of England, who met a mysterious death in the New Forest in 1100, and Thomas Becket, Archbishop of Canterbury, who was murdered in his cathedral in 1170. The question to be discussed in these pages is the nature of the evidence which makes such an hypothesis tenable.

This curious inquiry, involving as it does theology, philosophy, anthropology, and history, and touching each at controversial points, imposes a discipline of simplification. The primitive culture-pattern, the interaction of ancient civilizations and religions, the assumptions underlying astrology, the doctrines of Plato and the mysteries of Mithra, Catholic orthodoxy and early heresies, the problems of the Fourth Gospel and the Apocalypse, the meaning of Manicheism, the nature of Eros, the connection between the Albigenses and he Troubadours and the relationship of both to the medieval witch-cult—to mention only the main strands in the thread— are subjects which, in their own right, invite the seeker to lose himself in a labyrinth. But if any conclusion is to be reached, attention must be devoted to the thread and not to the labyrinth. Though the specialist in each section, versed in its complex detail, may deplore what must seem to him a most meagre outline, it is to be hoped that he will, remembering that any synthesis necessitates simplification, refrain from passing too harsh a judgement.

Particularly in dealing with the historical circumstances of the deaths of Rufus and Becket is emphasis laid on one factor only, because that factor alone is relevant to the thesis. The political economic and personal feuds and necessities, which are ordinarily accepted as in themselves sufficient to explain the occurrences, have their part in the whole picture. Certainly they influenced, in their several ways, the over-riding action. No event is as simple as it seems, least of all any 'historical' event. But in this case, for it to be seen at all it must be seen simply. And, if the sacrificial death be admitted as a factor (even though disagreement remains as to whether or not it was the determining factor) the general historical interpretation will not thereby be destroyed, but only added to and deepened.

As I have said, the object of this essay is not to prove a case, but to select and co-ordinate certain evidence which may suggest that there is a case to be proved. Adequately to sustain it would need a new *Golden Bough* written by scholars in co-operation, each specialist contributing those facts in his own field which are germane to the general inquiry. This only offers a tentative point of contact.

2. *The Pre-Christian Empires: 1000 B.C.–A.D. 1*

At the outset, a simple chronological conspectus may be useful. Approximately four millennia separate us in the twentieth century A.D. from the day when Abraham left the great civilization of the Chaldaeans to journey westward (*c.* 2000 B.C.). For the conditions and beliefs prevailing at this time we rely mainly on the archaeologist and the anthropologist. Between the accession of David to the throne of Israel (*c.* 1016 B.C.) and the death of William Rufus (A.D. 1100) are, roughly, two millennia, during which we are in the period of written history. The birth of Christ, marking the beginning of our era, stands at the centre, making an easily remembered, symmetrical division. The inquiry will be concerned mainly with the middle period, the thousand years before and the thousand years after the birth of Christ.

In the first thousand of these years, it is convenient to remember the dominant powers. At the beginning of them, the three civilizations of Chaldaea, Egypt and the 'Mycenaean' age in Crete were ending, and Assyria was the rising empire. In Judaea, Solomon was founding his temple which was to become the focus of a national religion (975) and in Greece the Homeric epics were giving the country a common theology and a common literary language (*c.* 950–750).

At the end of the first quarter of this millennium, Assyria, under Sennacherib, attained undisputed pre-eminence (750–700), but in 600 the power passed again to the Chaldaeans and the Chaldaean Nebuchadnezzar rebuilt the city and founded the new Babylonian empire. The period from 750 to 600 was the time of the colonizing activity of Greece which brought her into contact with the Mediterranean regions and, in particular, with Sicily and North Africa. In Judaea, the opening of it was the age of Isaiah and the close the beginning of the Exile (597).

9

The next hundred years was the century of Persia, under Cyrus, who captured Babylon (538), and his successor Darius, who organized the Persian empire—the first the world had seen which could reasonably claim to be universal.

It is in the Persia of 500 B.C. that much that is relevant to our inquiry is to be found, for 'the Persians learned from other nations to make images of their gods; and beside the supreme God, Ormuzd, other figures, such as the sun-god Mithra, gained an increasing hold. Their religion spread westward, notably in Cappadocia and Armenia. The Persian policy was one of strict tolerance and often the government definitely sought support among the priests of the native religions. In Babylon, Cyrus succeeded to the throne of the native kings and ruled as the "chosen of Marduk". The Babylonian priests, known as the Chaldaeans, with their mythical histories, their astrology and their astronomy, exercised a profound influence on the empire and, through it, on the history of the world.'[1]

But in 480 the defeat of the Persians by the Greeks at the battle of Salamis heralded the golden age of Greece. The unequalled century between Pericles (d. 429) and Alexander the Great (d. 323) saw the zenith of Greek philosophy in Plato and the widespread diffusion of Hellenistic culture in the wake of Alexander's conquest of the East.

During the next hundred years the focus shifted farther west where Rome struggled for the supremacy of the Mediterranean with Carthage, the powerful commercial empire in North Africa, originally founded by the Phoenicians of Tyre and Sidon about the time of the Jewish Exile. On the final defeat of Carthage in 202, Rome prepared herself for the founding of that empire which was to endure for five centuries.

Before, however, Rome made herself mistress of the world she had to try conclusions once more with the East. About the year 100 an energetic ruler of the regions about the Black Sea, Mithradates Eupator (whose name betokened his allegi-

[1] Mattingly: *Outline of Ancient History* (1914).

ance to the god Mithra) seemed for a while to give promise of being a second Alexander and founding another vast Asiatic empire. He shook the Roman hold on the East in a way which no contemporaries had imagined possible, and his final defeat by Pompey (65 B.C.) was, seen in historical perspective, as crucial as the deliverance from Carthage.

Then, in the year 12 B.C., Augustus (who, after the violent deaths of Pompey, Julius Caesar and Antony became the first of the Roman emperors) was proclaimed *pontifex maximus* and, in 2 B.C., *pater patriae*. Under its High Priest and Father, the *pax Romana* had begun. And Christ was born.

The millennium before His birth may thus be divided into its four quarters. During the first quarter, the dominant civilization was the Assyrian—a culture largely Semite and showing characteristics of the 'Jewish' type. During the second, the Persian, of Indo-European origin. During the third the Greek, and during the fourth the Roman. The importance of Assyria was that, by her very destructiveness which stamped out distinct nationalities in a large part of the Nearer East, she prepared the way for a cosmopolitan civilization in which not race but religion was the principal force. Into this inheritance, which each improved, her successors entered. Their centres, which have become symbols, were (the restored) Babylon, Athens and Rome. But it was to the capital of a small and much-warred-upon province that the roads of history and symbolism ultimately led—that Jerusalem which had survived the vicissitudes of the thousand years.

3. The Stream of Heresy: A.D. 40–A.D. 1000

In the thousand years after Christ, the chronology which concerns our purpose refers, in the main, to the movements of the Church and heresy. For the first 250 years the Christians in the Roman Empire had to face persecution. The same period saw the triumph of Mithraism, which had overrun the West from Cilicia, where it had been introduced by the remnants of the Pontic armies and fleets after Pompey's defeat of Mithradates. In A.D. 274 the Emperor Aurelian conferred official recognition on this cult of the *Unconquerable Sun* by founding the Temple of Sol Invictus and giving its priests precedence even over the members of the ancient Collegium Pontificum; though, in practice, toleration had been given from the beginning of the era (Tiridates of Armenia worshipped Nero (54–68) as an emanation of Mithra himself), and effective support since the end of the second century when the Emperor Commodus (180–192) was admitted into the Mithraic mysteries.

Faced outwardly by this rival, orthodox Christianity had to face the internal divisions caused by the various Gnostic heresies. Gnosticism sprang essentially from the same root as Mithraism and can be traced to the same Persian origin. Christian Gnosticism grew side by side with 'orthodox' Christianity and, in many instances, was inseparably intertwined with it.[1] Its most memorable form was Manichaeism in the third century. And 'the great Gnostic thinkers were heretics, not in the sense that they left the high road, but in the sense that the track along which they went was not the direction along which the high road was afterwards constructed'.[2]

If the Gnostic doctrines within the Church itself formed an underlying link with Mithraism, the outward expression of the two faiths had such remarkable similarities that they formed a matter for astonished comment from the times of their contemporaries till the present day, and St. Augustine himself has declared: 'I remember the priests of the fellow in the cap (illius pileati) used at one time to say "Our Capped One (i.e. Mithra) is himself a Christian".'[3]

Thus when the last great persecution of the Christians occurred under Diocletian in 303, the actual situation went far to warrant Harnack's epigram that the two sides, Christianity

---

[1] Even, as we shall see later, in the New Testament itself.
[2] F. C. Burkitt: *Church and Gnosis* (1932).
[3] Homilies on St. John, Discourse VII.

and Paganism, had only one theology but two rival mythologies. Ten years later, Constantine the Great issued his edict of toleration, and Christianity, not Mithraism, became the official religion; but his coinage still bore the image of *Sol invictus* which could be interpreted according to their own predispositions by either side without acrimony.

The Church, however, once it had the certain support of the State could not tolerate its rival and in spite of the reintroduction of Mithraism by Julian the Apostate (331–363) it was exterminated by a persecution probably more ruthless and efficient than any that has been known in the Western world.

Yet its doctrine did not perish with it. The moment of its expiry—at the end of the fourth century—was, not fortuitously, the moment when Gnosticism, in its Manichaean form, suddenly expanded in the West. The tradition that the original founders of the sect had conversed in Persia with priests of Mithra involves a profound historic truth. Both Mithraism and Manichaeism had been born in the East; both derived from a synthesis of Babylonian mythology and Persian dualism; both absorbed Hellenic elements; with the result that, though Mithraism as an organized religion disappeared with catastrophic completeness, in Manichaeism 'the Mithraic doctrines were to withstand for centuries all persecutions and, rising again in a new form in the Middle Ages, were to shake once more the ancient Roman world'.[1]

The Roman Empire lasted for about a century after Constantine and during that time the Church consolidated its position and defined its faith in a series of Ecumenical Councils from that of Nicaea (325), the first, to that of Chalcedon (451), the fourth. At the former the Creed was formulated; at the latter, the orthodox doctrine of the two natures of Christ was enunciated as a counterblast to the Gnostic interpretation current in the Church at Alexandria. In the fifth century, also, the New Testament took its final form and

[1] F. Cumont: *The Mysteries of Mithra* (1903).

13

general agreement was reached as to which of its books were 'canonical'. In two other spheres of ecclesiastical development the fifth century was decisive. It saw the founding of monastic life, which for a thousand years was to appeal to medieval men and women as the highest earthly ideal; and it produced the two great writers whose speculations were to dominate theology throughout the Middle Ages—the African Augustine and the Syrian pseudo-Dionysius.

Augustine from the age of nineteen to thirty was a Manichaean and subsequently a neo-Platonist. He was converted to Christianity in 386, but it is a tenable hypothesis that he never entirely shed his early, formative beliefs. Certainly Manichaean teaching left an enduring impression on his mind and 'in the contrasted conceptions of *Civitas Dei* and *Civitas Mundi* there is a considerable reflection of the Manichee notion of the eternal realms of Light and Dark'.[1]

The so-called Dionysius the Areopagite was, as far as can be ascertained, a Syrian writer who flourished at the end of the fifth century and was intimately acquainted with the works of the great neo-Platonist Proclus, who occupied the chair of philosophy at Alexandria in 450 where he endeavoured to give point to his saying that 'the philosopher should be the hierophant of the whole world' by celebrating Egyptian and Chaldaean, as well as Greek festivals. Between the works of Proclus and the pseudo-Dionysius there is an extraordinary parallelism—the Dionysian *De divinis nominibus*, for example, is little more than a transcript of Proclus's *De malorum substantia*—and it has even been contended that the pseudo-Dionysius was, in fact, a pagan priest. The general consensus of opinion of those who have studied his writings is that he was certainly not a Christian, though he had an intimate acquaintance with Christian thought and a command of Christian terminology. The probable Neo-Platonism of the Areopagite is of capital importance to the understanding of the medieval confusion, because in the Church the Dionysian

[1] F. C. Burkitt: *The Religion of the Manichees* (1925).

writings were regarded 'even as sacred'. The claim that they were written by Dionysius the Areopagite, the convert of St. Paul, was not disputed till the Renaissance and thus his pagan writings became the corner-stone of medieval scholasticism. 'The great masters of Saint-Victor at Paris, foremost among them the much-admired Hugh, based their teaching on the doctrine of Dionysius; Peter Lombard and the greatest Dominican and Franciscan scholars, Alexander of Hales, Albertus Magnus, Thomas Aquinas, Bonaventura, adopted his theses and arguments. Master poets like Dante and historians like Otto of Freising built on his foundations.'[1]

With the Dionysian and Augustinian writings entirely dominating the Church's thought, and monasticism (which was based on the fundamental Gnostic idea that the 'flesh' was 'evil') accepted as its ideal practice, the margin between orthodoxy and heresy was so slight as to be almost unnoticeable, and it was only when Gnosticism later ran to extremes that it was officially noticed. In the controversy about the two natures of Christ (which was its focal point theologically within the Church) both sides appealed to the Dionysian writings which were accommodatingly, if not intentionally, vague on the subject.

Thus, though their full development did not take place till later, all the factors which made for a universal religion—an authoritative church, an equivocal theology, a corpus of Sacred Writings, a uniform ideal for living—were present in the West in A.D. 500 as they had been in the Persian Empire of 500 B.C. The new Babylon had given place to the new Rome —and there were more ideas common to both than is apt to be admitted.

But the Old Religion—either nakedly in hiding or under the form of extreme Gnostic heresies claiming the Christian name—continued an existence independent of Catholic orthodoxy. In the middle of the seventh century occurred the

---

[1] J. Stiglmayr, s.j.: Art: 'Dionysius the Areopagite' in *Catholic Encyclopaedia*.

second diffusion of Manichaeism over Europe, when Constantius Sylvanus combined the doctrines of Zoroaster and St. Paul in what became known as Paulicianism. 'The new teacher easily united into one church the remnants of the old Gnostics, especially the Manichaeans of Armenia and the still unconverted Zoroastrians of Pontus and Cappadocia. Incessantly persecuted by the Byzantine powers, their chief, Carbeas, founded a new capital for his sect, the impregnable Tephrice, in the mountains near Trebizond; but which was ultimately destroyed by Basil the Macedonian about the year A.D. 880.'[1]

Their influence, however, was not confined to their capital. About A.D. 750 a colony of them was transplanted into depopulated Thrace, where their numbers were augmented in the tenth century by a fresh reinforcement drawn from the Chalybean hills. 'Here their missionaries converted the neighbouring pagans, the Bulgarians, whence the sect derived a new and more odious appellation, one which in course of time from denoting heresy in religion was fixed to the branding of heresy in love.'[2]

These Paulicians—or 'Bulgars'—warlike and fearless, enlisted in the Byzantine armies and were especially prominent in the wars with the Normans in Sicily. From this island they diffused their doctrines over Italy, gained converts even in Rome, and spread with even more rapidity over the south of France.

Here, in Provence, their influence, aided by that of the Gnostic 'Priscillianists' of Spain, led to a movement, the Albigenses or Cathars (the 'Pure') with their 'Church of Love', which was as great a menace to the medieval Church as Mithraism had been to the early Church and which was eventually exterminated (in the Albigensian crusade) with a ferocity inferior only to that which had characterized the rooting-out of Mithraism itself.

[1] C. W. King: *The Gnostics and their Remains* (1887).
[2] Ibid, This latter point is of some relevance to our inquiry and is treated further in the chapter on 'The Nature of Love'.

16

The 'believers' of the Catharist church and the bards of its heresy were the Troubadours; the Order of the Templars was later founded on doctrine which, if not exactly similar, was drawn from the same original source; and, in the early stages of the movement, it was almost impossible to discover the dividing line between it and orthodoxy, so deeply had the Gnostic ideas, which it expressed in a pure form, permeated the Church itself.

In the year 1056, the Synod of Toulouse condemned the Cathar Church as heretical. In the same year, William Rufus was born.

.   .   .   .   .

This intentionally brief and limited survey has excluded mention of such historically important events as the rise of Mohammedanism in the seventh and eighth centuries, with its direct and open menace to Christianity; the division of the Church itself into Eastern and Western; and the struggle between the Papacy and the Empire, because these happenings and their consequences, though they inevitably influenced the trend we are tracing, are not vital to the understanding of it.

To explain Rufus's opposition to the Church and Becket's opposition to the State in terms of the Papal-Imperial struggle is to adopt the conventional—and, if not untenable, at least unsatisfying—interpretation which may be found in any history book. That it was a factor in the situation, no one would attempt to deny; but underlying it were motives and beliefs altogether different and, at first sight, fantastic.

To state baldly that a King and a Primate of England were, within seventy years of each other, the self-immolated victims of a cult which preserved the rites of the primitive fertility ritual is to invite derision. But when the nature of the civilization in which they lived is more fully understood, when the channels of the transmission of the cult practices are perceived and, above all, when it is realized that behind the apparent crudity was a philosophy and a religion not so very

17

far removed from current orthodoxy, the matter may appear somewhat more credible.

But before examining the historical circumstances and their meaning, it is necessary to return far into the past to discover what the 'ritual pattern' of the cult was and how it had manifested itself in the religious practices of the two most ancient civilizations of Egypt and Babylonia centuries before Abraham left Ur.

Chapter II

THE CULTURE PATTERN AND THE CULT

1. The Blood Sacrifice

The researches of various schools of anthropologists, following in the tracks of Tyler's *Primitive Culture* and Frazer's *Golden Bough* (though not necessarily accepting all the conclusions of those classics) have established with some degree of certainty the nature of the primitive culture pattern and the myth and ritual expressive of it.

At the heart of it lies the Blood Sacrifice—'the priest who slew the slayer and shall himself be slain'.

From archaeological evidence it may be deduced that the blood offering goes back to the pre-agricultural stage of civilization and is the expression of man the hunter. Blood was the life-essence—the soul-substance common alike to man and to animals; for in primitive man there is no 'sharp line of distinction such as we see between man and other animals'.[1] The possession of this common vitality implied a mysterious bond between those who shared the life-essence. Moreover, its potency could be transmitted from one person or animal to another, so that renewed health could be secured by the—at first, actual: later, ritual—transference of soul-substance.

'In the ritual shedding of blood, it is not the taking of life, but the giving of life that is really fundamental, for blood is not death but life. The outpouring of the vital fluid in actuality, or by substitute, is the sacred act whereby life is given to

[1] Im Thurn: *Among the Indians of Guiana* (1883).

19

promote and preserve life, and to establish thereby a bond of union with the supernatural order. This seems to have been the primitive conception out of which an elaboration of ritual and belief has emerged, involving notions of the re-animation of human gods by the immolation of animal and human quasi-divine victims, and vegetation offerings, on the one hand; and, on the other hand, lofty ethical ideals of surrender, renunciation and self-sacrifice.'[1]

It would seem that the ritual killing of animals preceded human sacrifice, for, in a hunting state of culture, men depended for life itself on the animals round them. It was the animal, not the man, who was the god. If primitive man, sharing the animal life-essence 'was conscious of a unity of life uniting him in a mystic and irrational manner to the source of his food-supply', he also realized that 'to kill and eat a species so closely akin to a man's own nature and in many respects superior to him in strength and wisdom is an anomaly calling forth an emotional situation to be approached by an appropriate ritual'.[2]

Thus, at the beginning of things, both the Killing of the God and the Sacred Meal, which gave natural and supernatural strength from the partaking of his body and blood, were ritual acts with a mystical significance.

It is necessary to insist on this because the common idea of animal sacrifice as a later and more 'civilized' substitute for human sacrifice entirely misses the point of it. Also, it is essential to the understanding of the central Mithraic myth. In this myth—though, of course, it did not take its final form till thousands of years later and contains elements of vegetation ritual, sun worship, the Divine King and the metaphysical principles of good and evil—the expression of these primitive beliefs is very apparent.

According to this myth, the Bull was the first created living creature. On the mountain-side, the god Mithra seized it by

---

[1] E. O. James: *Origins of Sacrifice* (1933).
[2] Ibid.

its horns and succeeded in mounting it. The infuriated animal struggled in vain to free itself, but when it was exhausted by its efforts Mithra dragged it by its hind hooves over a road strewn with obstacles into the cave in which he was living on earth. Later the Bull escaped from the cave and once more roamed the mountain pastures. Thereupon the Sun sent a messenger—a raven—to command Mithra to slay the Bull. Much against his will, Mithra carried out this sacrilegious mission. He overtook the Bull just as it was taking refuge in the cave it had left, and killed it with his hunting knife. Immediately a miracle happened. From the dead body of the Bull sprang all the useful herbs and plants. From its spinal cord sprang the wheat, from its blood, the vine.[1] Its seed, gathered and purified by the Moon, produced all the species of useful animals; and its soul ascended into Heaven where, receiving the honours of divinity, it became Silvanus, the god of gardens, lover of the beautiful youth, Cyparissus. 'Thus, through the sacrifice which he had so resignedly undertaken, the tauroctonous hero became the creator of all the beneficent things on earth; and from the death which he had caused was born a new life.'[2]

2. *The Human Victim*

Second only in importance and antiquity to the blood-sacrifice of the hunter was the vegetation offering of the agri-culturist. And as the former was associated pre-eminently with the male principle, so was the latter with the female. Paleolithic data have established the existence of a cult of the female principle for the promotion of life in which effigies composed of newly-cut seedlings of corn, rye, maize or rice are conspicuous in agricultural ceremonial.[3] The best-known of such manifestations is probably the 'corn-maiden', made

[1] Bull's blood is still used to fertilize vines.
[2] Cumont: op. cit.
[3] Frazer *Golden Bough* (1914), pt. vii: 'Spirits of the Corn and of the Wild.'

from the last sheaf garnered, which forms to-day a still recognizable link between our own times and the earliest dawn of pre-history.

As vegetation is the offspring of the Great Mother Earth and, for that reason, 'is animated by quasi-divine soul-substance analogous to that which the animals share with man, a similar paradoxical situation exists in agricultural communities as among hunting tribes'.[1] The crops are the means of life, yet their very 'sacredness' makes them dangerous unless they are approached with ritualistic apology. How inevitably the two rituals became fused may, perhaps, best be seen from the practice of the Matabele where the chief sacrifices a bull before the tomb of his grandfather and deposits pots of fresh beer and porridge made from the first-fruits of the earth in front of the shrine. The blood of the bull is then sprinkled on the carefully-weeded and freshly-ploughed soil and a feast on the carcass, the porridge and the beer follows.

There seems to be, however, a difference in purpose behind the meal which followed the blood sacrifice and that which followed the vegetation offering, in so far as they were distinct. The partaking of the body of the animal was directed primarily to the transference of the vital energy; the ritual eating of the first-fruits was mainly a device to enable them to be consumed without injury either to the recipients or to the vegetative processes. The first was a 'sacrament' in the sense that the second was not. But it was from the second, which focused attention on the yearly cycle and the death, the resurrection and the life of vegetation, that there arose the complex myth and ritual pattern on which 'civilization' was founded.

As this civilization first arose in Egypt and Babylonia, both of which depended on rivers for their fertility, it was natural that the Earth, as the Great Mother, should find in a river-god her male counterpart and consort. The Sumerian Ishtar has as her son-lover Tammuz, originally typified by life-giving

[1] James: op. cit.

waters. The Egyptian Isis had in Osiris, identified with the life-giving Nile, her brother-spouse.

But there was another element in the vegetation ritual, especially in the Nile Valley—the Sun, whose power was an insistent fact which could hardly be overlooked and demanded entry into any system based on an interpretation of natural phenomena. Inevitably the Sun became the centre of the sacrificial system and gradually drew to itself the ideas concerning the other offerings. It was the life-giving principle. It had, in the heavens, the superiority which distinguished the Great Bull among animals. Like the fruits of the earth, it had its rhythmic death and resurrection. The myths of man— which are the 'book of the words' of the ritual—eventually came to be traced in the stars, and at springtime the Sun rose in the sign of the Bull.

As early as the Fourth Dynasty of Egypt (c. 3000 B.C.) there was a solar line of kings reigning from Heliopolis, the City of the Sun, and the human community was linked with the supra-mundane powers by the fiction that the Pharaoh was one manifestation of the Sun God and that, at his death, he was translated to the realms of his heavenly counterpart.

It was from this background of belief and practice that the idea of human sacrifice sprung. The pattern has intricacies and variations innumerable; both chronologically in time and geographically in place, it has characteristic modifications; but in essence it remains the recognized ritual device for perpetuating the life of the world. The King embodies the 'psychic whole' of the community; he also embodies the divine source of all life. Therefore he must not be allowed to become old or ill, lest his diminishing vigour affect adversely the community and the crops on which it depends. He must die so that, in his resurrection, both God and man may live.

3. *The Pattern and the Myths*

The ritual pattern, which we find already highly developed

in the Egypt and Babylonia of 3000 B.C., represents the things done to and by the king in order to secure the prosperity of the community for the coming year, and behind the dramatic representation of the death and resurrection of the king lies the original custom of sacrificially killing him.

Both in Egypt and in Babylonia the king represented the god in the seasonal rituals; and in the annual festival the following elements were to be found—the dramatic mime of the god's death and resurrection; the recitation (or ritual representation) of the creation myth; the combat, showing the triumph of the god over his enemies; the sacred marriage; and the triumphal procession.

'These elements might vary in different localities and at different periods, some being more strongly stressed than others, but they constitute the underlying skeleton, so to speak, not only of such seasonal rituals as the great New Year festivals, but also of coronation rituals, initiation rituals, and may even be discerned in occasional rituals, such as spells against demons and various diseases.'[1]

It is outside the scope of this essay to discuss in detail the profound influence which this ritual pattern has had on the development of civilization. There is a library of books on the subject[2] and it can be contended with much reason that 'civilization' itself is the product of it. It is at least in this sense and with this implication that in these pages the words 'culture pattern' are used. In one sense, 'religion' and 'civilization' are two aspects of the same phenomenon. There is unity at the source; the community and the cosmos move to the same rhythm.

Into the pattern, at various points of it, the great myths are seen to fit—the death and resurrection of Tammuz and Osiris and Attis; the Bull sacrifice in Mithraism and in the religion of the Mycenaean age of Crete (of which the Minotaur re-

[1] S. H. Hooke: 'The Myth and Ritual Pattern of the Ancient East', in *Myth and Ritual* (1933).

[2] See, in particular, A. M. Hocart: *Kingship* (1927).

mains the symbol); the passion of Aleion, son of Baal. In the creation myths and the combat accompanying it, we see the struggle between Horus and Set in Egypt, Marduk and Tiamat in Babylon, Ormuzd and Ahriman in Persia, Yahweh and the Dragon in Israel. In the myths of the Sacred Marriage are all the stories of the goddess of fertility and love, be she worshipped as Isis or Ishtar or Astarte or Aphrodite. In the eventual triumph of the god is the climax of all theologies as well as the 'happy ending' of all fairy tales.

Yet though it may be necessary to know something of the inter-relation of the myths (and the ritual which they explain) in order to realize the 'popular' religious idiom of any community, the more important factors are, first, their origin, with its emphasis on blood, and, secondly, their application to the personal problems of the individual by way of philosophical interpretation and esoteric initiation. For life and death, good and evil, the nature of love, the impulse to create and the necessity to struggle towards success (however 'success' be defined) remain the eternal problems of the individual. So much are they within the terms of the pattern that there are some who maintain that the pattern itself is capable of psycho-analytic interpretation. Such a view, though it is untenable in its extreme form, is valuable in that it emphasizes the unity underlying the bewildering diversity and explains in part the validity of the pattern, in one or other of its interpretations, for all men at all stages of development.

4. The Mysteries

According to Professor Elliot Smith, 'in delving into the remotely distant history of our species we cannot fail to be impressed with the persistence with which, throughout the whole of his career, man (of the species *sapiens*) has been seeking for an elixir of life to give added "vitality" to the dead (whose existence was not consciously regarded as ended) to prolong his own life from all assaults not merely of time, but also of circumstance. In other words the elixir he sought was something that would bring "good luck" in all the events of his life and its continuation. Most of the amulets, even of modern times, the lucky trinkets, the averters of the "Evil Eye", the practices and devices for securing good luck in love and sport, in curing bodily ills and mental distress, in attaining material prosperity or a continuation of existence after death, are survivals of the ancient and persistent striving after those objects which our earliest forefathers called collectively the "givers of life".[1]

But whereas the vast majority of men, then and now, contented themselves with superficialities, there have always been those whose temperament drives them deeper, either intellectually or emotionally, into the search for the Thing which shall give them effective power in this world and the next whether that Thing be conceived as the Elixir of Life or the Philosopher's Stone or the unuttered and unutterable Word or merely a Way of Life.

It was this need that brought into existence the secret initiatory cults which promised this knowledge to their devotees. And for those whose approach was intellectual rather than emotional, there was philosophy. But both the philosopher and the initiate were bound by the presuppositions of the culture-pattern, the one because its concepts, however outrageous they might sometimes appear, were rooted in reality; the other because, as a microcosm of the community, their initiatory rituals preserved the pattern itself. The Initiate was the King.

In the initiation rites of the most famous Egyptian cult, for example, in so far as they can be reconstructed, the novice underwent a ceremonial sanctification which was celebrated as a sacramental drama with an elaborate death and resurrection ritual, for the purpose of ensuring his salvation when he rose from a mystic grave. Before his initiation he underwent various trials of endurance and during the time he was 'dead'

[1] Elliot Smith: *Evolution of the Dragon* (1919).

'was borne through all the elements'.[1] Next morning he stood before the congregation arrayed in sacramental garments in the likeness of the solar deity with whom he was identified—that is to say, he had passed through the experience of death in union with the Sun-God.

If the death-resurrection *motif* was that most stressed by the cults, it was the combat which was emphasized by the philosophers, whose main preoccupation was the problem of Good and Evil. Their elaboration of this theme, with their acceptance of or attempt to escape from dualism, interacted with the initiatory quest for life through death, and resulted in the paradox of a movement (through Gnosticism, Manichaeism and Catharism) whose ritual was derived from the practices intended to secure life yet which at the same time considered procreation as the ultimate evil.

To understand this 'secret of the cult', it will be necessary to consider in somewhat more detail the nature of these doctrines.

[1] Apuleius: *Metamorphoses*.

Chapter III

THE METAMORPHOSES OF MITHRA

---

1. Persia and Babylon

The origin of Mithra is lost in obscurity. All that can be asserted is that 'in that unknown epoch when the ancestors of the Persians were still united with those of the Hindus, they were already worshippers of Mithra. The hymns of the Vedas celebrated his name, as did those of the Avesta, and despite the differences obtaining between the two theological systems of which these books are the expressions, the Vedic Mitra and the Iranian Mithra have preserved so many traits of resemblance that it is impossible to entertain any doubt concerning their common origin.'[1] In both, he is the god of light, in the physical sense; and, in the moral, the protector of truth and the opponent of error. But as his early development as well as his eventual triumph was in his Persian rather than in his Indian context, it is best to connect him with the Avesta.

The distinguishing mark of this Persian religion, which is associated with the name of Zoroaster, is its dualism. Ormuzd, the 'living creator', the 'all-wise Lord', the 'source of light for the world', the 'father of all rectitude' is opposed at every point by his twin, Ahriman, the 'hurtful spirit', the 'evil mind', the 'demon of destruction'. These primeval brothers were said to have chosen between the good and evil, the right and the wrong which, apparently, existed before them in the very nature of things.

Between them takes place the Great Combat for the pos-

[1] Cumont: op. cit.

session of the universe. The stars in their courses fight for Ormuzd; the forces of destruction in the elements, the *devas*, for Ahriman. The conflict is endless for though it was at all times believed that Ormuzd *would* eventually defeat Ahriman —that Life would conquer Death—it was never asserted that the victory *had* occurred. Ormuzd was the supreme god, throned in high heaven; by obedience to his precepts the believer could share his life. But he was not lord of Ahriman. Ahriman, no less than Ormuzd, was a creator.

'The Iranian Satan was no Lucifer fallen from Heaven to play the rebel against God, on a throne of desperation and under omnipotent thunderbolts of doom—but an invisible Presence, armed with personal power equal to his hate of good, infecting alike the outward and the inward worlds.'[1] The Avesta has no philosophy of evil. How evil and death originated and their relationship to good and life do not enter into the question. Everything centres in the divided will. As Ormuzd says to Ahriman: 'Neither our thoughts, doctrines, wills, vows, words, acts, laws nor our souls agree.'

In the warfare between the twins, the great champion of Ormuzd is Mithra who, in the Avesta, is simply the genius of celestial light. But, in course of time, he became identified with the Sun itself and, in the popular mind, was almost synonymous with Ormuzd. It was said that Ormuzd created Mithra as great and worthy as himself and 'established him to maintain and watch over all this moving world'.

His mediatorial capacity, however, became more important than his apparent identity as the thought of men emphasized the infinity of God; and the final picture was one which showed Ormuzd, enthroned in an empyrean above the stars ('as far above the sun as the sun is distant from the earth') where perpetual serenity exists; below him, an active deity, Mithra, his emissary and chief of the celestial armies in their ceaseless combat with Ahriman who, from the bowels of Hell, under the earth, sends forth his *devas* to the surface.

[1] Johnson: *Oriental Religions: Persia* (1885).

As Persia came into contact with Babylon, so on the primitive Zoroastrian belief was imposed the erudite theology of the Chaldeans, with their worship of the stars and their astronomical knowledge. The legends and divinities of the two religions were assimilated. Ormuzd was confounded with Bel (the Baal of the Old Testament) who reigned over the heavens, while Mithra became the Sun, Shamash—who, like Mithra in Persia, was also god of justice. The great combat, in Babylonian mythology, was between Marduk (Bel-Merodach) the creator and Tiamat (Mummu Tiawath, the sea and first creatress, 'mother of all living') who assembled the powers of evil, bringing forth dragons and serpents.

Here, in this Babylonian version of the combat, the interpretation differs on an essential point from the Zoroastrian. Good and evil are not regarded as two equal and contemporary powers. Evil comes first and the story centres in the wish of the Goddess of the powers of evil to retain creation in her own hands. But the conflict ended in the triumph of Bel-Marduk who defeated and dismembered Tiamat and, having made a covering for the heavens with half the body of the defeated Dragon of Chaos, ordered the world anew and created man with his own blood, in order that the service and worship of the gods might be established.

Echoes of the killing of Tiamat are found, still recognizable enough, in the Bible—in the seventy-fourth Psalm, where God is praised because: 'Thou didst divide the sea by thy strength; thou brakest the heads of the dragons in the waters: thou brakest the heads of Leviathan in pieces'; in the fifty-first chapter of Isaiah, with its invocation: 'Awake, awake, put on strength, O arm of the Lord; awake as in the ancient days, in the generations of old. Art thou not it that hath cut Rahab and wounded the dragon?'; in the Apocalypse and again in Isaiah, where the past tradition is expressed in the form of futurity: 'And there was war in heaven: Michael and his angels fought against the dragon; and the dragon fought and his angels, and prevailed not; neither was their place found any more in heaven. And the great dragon was cast out, that old serpent called the Devil and Satan, which deceiveth the whole world' (Rev. xii, 7) and 'In that day, the Lord with his sore and great and strong sword shall punish Leviathan the piercing serpent, even Leviathan that crooked serpent; and he shall slay the dragon that is in the sea' (Isa. xxvii, 1). And there are many more which will be familiar enough to the student.

2. The Host of Heaven

The Babylonians introduced, however, another line of approach into the composite religion. From long and tabulated observation of the stars, the Magi had established the invariability of the sidereal revolution and from this had deduced two ideas. The first was the existence of a Necessity, to which the gods as well as men were subject, in that it controlled their movements. The second was the eternity of the world, for the stars perform their revolutions according to an invariable cycle of years which succeed each other to infinity.

Depending from these two ideas was a third—the sacred properties of numbers. For the heavenly bodies, by their regular movements, taught man to divide into successive sections the unbroken chain of moments. Thus each of the periods marked in the unending flight of time, particularly the four seasons, shared the divinity of the stars. The number four seems from the beginning to have had a peculiar significance in numerology and, as it is one of the strands in the thread of our labyrinth, it may be conveniently outlined here.

To understand it, it is necessary to lay aside all modern mathematical approaches (which naturally see in the veneration expressed throughout antiquity for the four a mere childish fantasy), and accept the eminently 'unscientific' theories of addition and reduction.

By reduction is meant the reducing of all numbers formed

of more than one figure to the number of a single figure by the addition of the digits. Thus $15=1+5=6$; $743=7+4+3=14=1+4=5$, and so on. By addition is meant ascertaining the value of a number by adding together all the figures from unity to itself inclusively. Thus $6=1+2+3+4+5+6=21$, which by reduction $(2+1)$ equals 3. And $4=1+2+3+4=10=1$.

The combination of these two processes reduces any number to a single number between 1 and 3, and 4 returns to unity again; and it is precisely this quality of the number 4 which gave it its significance. It was both the expression of Unity and the point of transition back to unity. 1 was conceived as the active principle, 2 as the passive, 3 as the neuter; and the principles lead to the 4 which represents a new acceptance of the Unity as an active principle.

Here is one clue to the identification of 4 with God in a special and specialized sense which, in the Christian era, was to become the hall-mark of heresy. Four was the transition from the metaphysical to the physical, in a sense closely resembling the meaning of 'the Word made Flesh'.

Meanwhile, in Greece, Pythagoras—a contemporary of Cyrus of Persia—was engaged in those researches which have given him the title of 'the father of mathematics' and founding the Pythagorean brotherhood whose beliefs corresponded with some exactitude with those of Persian dualism—regarding the body as the 'tomb' of the soul, inculcating a strict asceticism and offering initiates, by the esoteric doctrines, an escape from 'the wheel of life'. If the modern world tends to separate the 'science' from the 'superstition', it does so at the expense of understanding either the aims or the teaching of the great Greek who 'of all men was the most assiduous inquirer' and who found reason to believe that 'all things are numbers'.

The Pythagorean interpretation of the number 4 differed in some respects from what seems to have been the Chaldean, but attached no less importance to it. Four was identified with Justice because it was the first square number, the product of equals. As representative of the solid (as 1 was of the point, 2 of the line and 3 of the surface), it had a mystical 'creative' significance. And the 'Holy Tetraktys', by which the Pythagoreans used to swear, was a triangular figure on a

base of four, thus: indicating at a glance the $1+2+3$

$+4=10=1$ principle which we have already noticed in the other numerological method.

The number, indeed, found its place in other contemporary religions. 'Egyptian incense was made out of sixteen ingredients and so furnished an impressive testimony to the Pythagorean admiration for the number four; Jewish incense was at least made of four ingredients and could therefore claim to prove that Judaism was acquainted with this part of the wisdom of Pythagoras.'[1] But the most obvious symbolical use of it is in a book written in Babylon about the time of Pythagoras's birth (and based therefore on the Chaldaean not on the Greek approach) to which reference can be made by everybody—the first chapter of the Old Testament Book of Ezekiel. Here in the description of the Divine Chariot and its rider, the prominent theme of the book, are the four living creatures, with four faces and four wings, and the four wheels in which is their spirit. Undoubtedly the 'Chariot' theme was older than Ezekiel and was charged with a significance which was understood by the initiates of the cult in all its forms—a significance which survived through the centuries and still survives in the seventh card of the Tarot, 'The Chariot'. This 'card gives the key to the whole Tarot, is dominated by the symbols of the quaternary in all its acceptations' and 'shows the influence of the creation in the preservation of the Divine in the Human'.[2]

[1] W. L. Knox: *St. Paul and the Church of the Gentiles* (1939).
[2] Papus: *The Tarot of the Bohemians* (1914).

33

The connection between the 4, which is the Pythagorean 'Justice' and Mithra in his aspect of god of justice is an obvious, if somewhat superficial, analogy—superficial because the implications of the 'four' symbolism go much deeper. There is, for example, the story of the raising of Lazarus (which appears only in the Gospel according to St. John) with its insistence that 'when Jesus came He found that he had lain in the grave four days already'. That this had a particular significance alike to the original writer and to his contemporaries, it is at least permissible to assume; the more so when we find that St. Augustine (who must have known, from his Manichaean days, its esoteric meaning) starts his commentary on the verse thus: 'Concerning the four days, many things, indeed, may be said, such being the case with the dark sayings of the Scripture, that, according to the diversity of the persons understanding them, they beget many senses.' His own interpretation—that Lazarus signifies all mankind and that the four days of death are birth (which has death implicit in it), the rejection of the natural law, the rejection of the Jewish Law and the rejection of the Gospel—may derive something from the doctrines he knew but would not reveal.[1] And there may be another clue in Plutarch's assertion in 'On the E at Delphi' that 'they that venerate the number Four do not ill to teach that by reason of this number every body has its origin'.

In the Christian era, indeed, the struggle of the Church with the Gnostic heretics might even be epitomized as the fight between the 3 and the 4—with the 3 used in a new and revolutionary sense as the Christian Trinity and the 4 retaining its old significance under the form of the 'Four-faced Father' who was the God of the Manichaeans and whom

---

[1] The whole chapter (John xi) raises many questions of esoteric interpretation. The ninth verse, for example: 'Jesus answered: Are there not twelve hours in the day? If any man walk in the day he stumbleth not' was always taken to support the astrological doctrine of elections. See Lynn Thorndike: *History of Magic and Experimental Science* (1923).

every convert to Christianity had formally to abjure. And when we come to the death of Becket, which took place—as the chroniclers date it—'on the fourth day before the Kalends of January' at four in the afternoon; was carried out by four blows delivered by four knights, with (according to one account) four other knights as witnesses, after the victim had ascended four steps, we find the *motif* of this number as inescapable as, without some knowledge of this background, it is meaningless.

But to return to the Chaldaeans, with whom the intricacies of numerology originated. Their contribution to the development of the ritual pattern was to impose on the primitive fertility festivals ideas derived from astrology and to systematize nature worship by a sidereal theology, which connected the power of nature with astronomical theories. So 'a vast pantheism inherited and codified the ideas of ancient animism. The eternal world is wholly divine, either because it is itself God or because it is conceived as containing within it a divine soul which pervades all things. The great reproach which Philo the Jew casts is precisely this—that they worship the creation instead of the Creator.'[1]

The worship was, however, given in the first place to Heaven—for here the concept of the Persians modified it—as the seat of the higher Powers. Among the stars, the most important was the moon, then the sun. (The primacy of the moon, which in all mythologies is feminine, may possibly be an echo of the first creation by Tiamat, especially since it is connected with the sea, which is the element of the Dragon-Creatress.) Next came the five planets, each of which was identified with a mythological deity. They were called 'Interpreters' because, since they have a particular movement not possessed by the fixed stars, they pre-eminently were held to manifest to man the purposes of the gods.

But 'all the host of Heaven' was also worshipped, and,

[1] Cumont: *Astrology and Religion among the Greeks and Romans* (1912).

more particularly, the twelve signs of the Zodiac, which were called the 'Counsellor Gods'. Then, outside the Zodiac, twenty-four stars, twelve in the Northern Hemisphere, twelve in the Southern (which were thus sometimes visible, sometimes invisible) which were the 'Judges' of the living and the dead.

The movements of the Heavens inevitably had their reactions upon Earth, but, above all, on the destiny of Man. The principle of life was of the same essence as the fires of heaven. From these the soul received its qualities at birth and, at that moment, the stars determined its fate on earth. Through Intelligence, which was divine, the soul could enter into relations with the gods. By contemplating the stars the faithful received from them the revelation of all knowledge and, after death, the knowledge-filled soul reascended to the divine stars and obtained immortality in the celestial abode.

Thus, to the Persian interpretation of the world in terms of Will, was added the Chaldaean conception of cosmic fatalism and stellar divination—an amalgam which was expressed in a mythology of bewildering intricacy.

3. The Stoics

Such, in its main outlines, was the religion which had its centre at Babylon about 500 B.C., where Cyrus the Persian, the 'chosen of Marduk', ruled the first world-empire.

In the struggle between Persia and Greece, which was so soon to follow, a further synthesis was to take place and, although the conquests of Alexander the Great were to impress the ideas of Greece on all Hither Asia, 'Iranism' never surrendered to Hellenism. If the West was outwardly triumphant, the theological victory remained with the East. From the sixth to the fourth century B.C., the whole marvellous development of Greek philosophy shows that it knew nothing of astrolatry and 'as long as Greece remained Greece, stellar divination gained no hold on the Greek mind and all attempts to substitute an astronomic theology for their immoral but charming idolatry were destined to certain failure'.[1]

But after the conquests of Alexander, a change took place. A cosmopolitan civilization demanded cosmopolitan gods and the stars, which were common to all men, came into their own. And while, on the one hand, Iranism introduced into Hellenism its astronomical ideas, on the other it strove to reconcile its popular deities. Ormuzd was identified with Zeus; the Bull was consecrated to Artemis; and Mithra, already regarded in Babylon as the peer of Shamash, was associated with Helios. The triumph of Mithra was sufficiently impressive to symbolize the victory of the East; for he was not only never subordinated to the native Helios, but his Persian name was never replaced in the liturgy by a translation, as was the case with the other divinities.

The triumph in popular religion was paralleled by the Eastern permeation of philosophy. At the beginning of the 'Alexandrine' period, Stoicism was founded by Zeno and whether or not Chaldaean doctrines contributed directly to Zeno's ideas, they exhibited a singular analogy to his pantheism, which represented Fire as the first principle and regarded the stars as the purest manifestation of its power.

Stoicism represented the world as a great organism, the 'sympathetic' forces of which acted and reacted, of necessity, on one another. It was thus bound to attribute a predominating influence to the celestial bodies, which were the most powerful in nature; and its 'Destiny' connected with the infinite succession of causes, readily agreed with the determinism of the Chaldaeans.

Even in common parlance the popular idea of the 'stoic' to-day, after two thousand years, is that of the good man, fatalistically pursuing his goodness in the face of the evil and pain of the world, with no guarantee of the ultimate triumph of the good; and thus its affinity can be seen with the phil-

[1] Cumont: *Astrology and Religion.*

osophy of an unfinished struggle between good and evil as expressed in the legend of Ormuzd and Ahriman.

4. The Logos

Also in the Stoic doctrine was a conception which had been handed down from earlier Greek pantheism—the term used by Heraclitus of Ephesus, a contemporary of Pythagoras, to denote the rule or law which governs the world-process, Logos, a cosmic, all-pervading principle of reason. As, for the Stoics, the ultimate world-substance was Fire, the controlling Reason of the universe is a fiery substance which contains within itself its own Logos, that is to say, the law of its own development and the explanation of all it becomes—a rational and divine law which may be called Nature or Necessity or Fate or Reason. For the Stoic the *summum bonum* was to live 'homologically' (i.e. a life according to Logos) for it was by possession of 'right Logos' as an indwelling deity that he could attain happiness.

The idea of Logos, the Stoic's World-Spirit or Reason of God immanent in creation, was taken over by Philo, an Alexandrian Jew who lived at the beginning of our era. Philo made it the basis of an elaborate philosophy, and culled from East and West every thought and idea relevant to his conception of a Vice-regent of God, a mediator between the Eternal and the ephemeral. 'His Logos reflects light from countless facets. It is one of those creative phrases, struck out in the crisis of projection, which mark an epoch in the development of thought.'[1]

In the hands of Philo, the Logos became the Wisdom of God, the Son of God, the Sun, an archangel of many names who was the leader and, in a sense, the creator of the host of heavenly beings, inferior to the Deity but superior to man. From the point of view of the world, the Logos is the Great Pattern, according to which it is made, as well as its Lord.

[1] Bigg: *The Christian Platonists of Alexandria* (1913).

'God with justice and law leads His great flock, the four elements and all that is shaped thereof, the circlings of Sun and Moon, the rhythmic dances of the Stars, having set over them His upright Word (Logos), His first-born Son, who will receive charge of this holy Flock as the Vice-regent of the Great King.'[1]

As regards Man, the Logos is both Saviour and Mediator and the Heavenly Man who, in the eyes of God, represents the whole family on earth. 'I stand', Philo makes him say, 'between the Lord and you, I who am neither uncreated like God nor created like you, but a mean between two extremes, a hostage to either side.'[2] And this division in the divine nature leads to a corresponding distinction in the spiritual life. To know God in His Powers is one thing: to know Him as He is in Himself is another and higher. This latter is the true Knowledge, the Gnosis, which brings Wisdom, Vision, Peace.[3]

Mankind is divided into two great classes—the godless whose guide is the lower intelligence; and the moral, spiritual man. The life of the spiritual man has two stages, that of the 'Babe', who knows God only in His powers, and that of the 'Perfect' who has attained the true Gnosis which leads to comprehension of the Logos.

It will be seen that, translated into terms of popular mythology, the philosophic Logos-doctrine was easily applicable to Mithra, with Gnosis as the secret of his initiates. And when the writer of the Fourth Gospel appropriated the Logos for Christ, there remained an equivocal flavour at least about his Prologue—those introductory verses of the Gospel according to St. John, in which the Logos-doctrine finds its greatest and most enduring expression.[4] By omitting verses 6–8 (a refer-

[1] Bigg: op. cit.

[2] *Quis rerum div. heres*, quoted in Bigg, op. cit.

[3] See also p. 70 for the connection of the Logos with 'Wisdom'.

[4] The modern fashion among commentators is to minimize the Philonic content of the Fourth Gospel—an attitude which is possibly dictated by a quite unnecessary fear of the conclusions to which such a premiss will lead. But the analogies are too patent to be explained away. See, for example, Bury: *The Fourth Gospel and the Logos-Doctrine* (1940).

ence to John the Baptist which are a necessary historical interpolation from the point of view of the Christian writer) the hymn reads thus:

In the beginning was the Word (Logos) and the Word was with God and the Word was God.
The same was in the beginning: with God.
All things were made by Him and without Him was not anything made that was made
In him was life; and the life was the Light of men.
And the Light shineth in darkness; and the darkness overcame it not.
That was the true Light, which lighteth every man that cometh into the world.
He was in the world and the world was made by Him and the world knew Him not (i.e. had not the true Gnosis)
He came unto His own and His own received Him not.
But as many as received Him to them gave He power to become Sons of God,
Even to them that believe on his name:
Which were born not of blood, nor of the will of the flesh, nor of the will of man, but of God.

Here, it will be at once seen, are the leading ideas with which we are already familiar—not only those of the Logos and Gnosis, but the opposition of Light and Dark (to be much elaborated a century later) as well as the power given to the initiate.

This 'Prologue' was eventually appointed by the Church as the Gospel for 25th December, which, as the winter solstice, was the birthday of the Invincible Sun, when Mithra was miraculously born in a cave and was first worshipped by shepherds. In the fourth century—that is to say, when the struggle between Mithraism and Christianity had been concluded in favour of the latter—25th December was made 'Christmas Day'.

In the eleventh and twelfth centuries—the centuries of

William Rufus and Thomas Becket—there was a further development in the liturgical use of these verses. They began to be said, in certain places, by the priest on his way back from the altar after Mass—a custom which gradually spread and resulted (though not till 1570) in a decree which made the reading of them after Mass obligatory in all Catholic churches, as it remains to this day.

Also in the eleventh and twelfth centuries, the reading or recital of them was the central rite of the heretical Albigenses, a circumstance which suggests the persistence of a dual significance, and which is of some pertinence to the last days of Becket.

5. The Gnostics

In considering briefly the Gnosticism of the second century DA.., it is not for our purpose necessary to enter into the question as to whether or not the 'Gnosis' was essentially an Eastern philosophy directly founded on the ideas we have been considering—as recent scholars such as Bossuet and Reitzenstein have held—or whether Burkitt[1] is right in returning to the traditional view that Gnosticism cannot properly be considered apart from the Christian system. The more probable hypothesis would seem to be that summed up by St. Augustine—who may be presumed to have known much more about the matter than any commentator of any succeeding age—when he wrote: 'That which is called the Christian Religion existed among the ancients, and never did not exist, from the beginning of the human race until Christ came in the flesh, at which time the true religion which already existed began to be called Christianity.'[2] The inescapable fact is that the heathen Gnostics, in the succession of Plutarch (one of the best examples of the cultivated Gnostic) and the Christian Gnostics, with whom the Fathers of the Church waged controversial war, started with the same prob-

[1] *Church and Gnosis* (1932).
[2] *Episcopi Retract*, Lib. I, c. XIII, 3.

41

lem, postulated the same premises and arrived at the same conclusion.

The problem was the nightmare of physical and moral evil and the way of salvation from it[1]; the hypothesis they accepted was the existence of a second and imperfect God, the Creator or Demiurge (in direct succession to Ahriman and Tiamat and—in the thought of the Christian Gnostics—identified with the Jehovah of the Old Testament); and the conclusion they reached was that only by leading a life devoted, positively, to Gnosis and, negatively, to the avoidance of giving hostages to the Demiurge could they obtain salvation.

'The grand doctrine of Gnosticism was this: The soul on being released from the body (its prison-house) has to pass through the regions of the Seven Powers; which it cannot do unless it is impregnated beforehand with knowledge (gnosis); otherwise it is seized upon and swallowed up by the dragon-formed ruler of this world and voided forth through its tail upon earth again, where it animates a swine or some such beast and repeats its career once more. But should it be filled with knowledge (gnosis) it eludes the Seven Powers and mounts up into the Eighth Heaven. Epiphanius quotes from the "Gospel of Philip" a formula intended to extort a free passage from the Planetary Genii: "The Lord hath revealed unto me what words the soul must use as it ascendeth up into Heaven, and how it must make answer to each one of the Celestial Virtues: ' I have known myself; I have collected myself from all parts, neither have I begotten sons to the Ruler of this World. I know thee who thou art, for thou art one from above.' But if convicted of having left any offspring upon earth, the soul is destined there until it shall have collected all and attracted these unto itself. . . . This 'Self-Collec-

---

[1] Cf. Francis Thompson's: 'Misery cries out to me from the kerb-stone, despair passes me by in the ways: I discern limbs laden with fetters impalpable but not imponderable . . . and I ask myself whether there be indeed an Ormuzd and an Ahriman, and whether Ahriman be the stronger of the twain.' F. Meynell: *The Life of Francis Thompson* (1913).

tion' was only to be effected through the observance of perpetual chastity, or rather (inevitable compromise) the practice of the various unnatural vices that regularly spring from such an article of faith. . . . The very plain-spoken Epiphanius gives exact particulars, not to be put into a modern tongue, of the mode in which the faithful observed in one sense their vow of perpetual chastity without renouncing the joys of Venus." [1]

According to Theodotus, the 'Spiritual', who soar up at once through the Seven Heavens to the Eighth Heaven— which is known as the Ogdoad—the region of the fixed stars where there is no more labour or change, are masculine, the children of Adam; the 'Psychic', the 'Called' are feminine, the children of Eve. (This distinction between Adam who is created by the spirit and Eve who is formed from Adam's flesh is recalled by St. Augustine in his commentary of the 'Prologue' to the Fourth Gospel.) The 'Spiritual' must be 'shaped' by gnosis; the Psychic must be 'grafted on to the fruitful olive', 'changed' from slavery into freedom, from feminine to masculine. Unless they become spiritual they can rise no higher than the fourth heaven (Paradise). They can become masculine only by union with the 'male angels' who love them and yearn for them as their spiritual brides and aid them to rise through the three remaining 'mansions' to the Ogdoad, their final home. [2]

A comparison between the beliefs of the Christian Gnostics within the second century Church and the elaborated doctrine of triumphant Mithraism in opposition to it goes far to explain why, for example, Hippolytus, Bishop of Portus, in his voluminous treatise *The Refutation of all Heresies* early in the third century should assert that the new Christian mysticism was merely the old Pagan Mysteries.

Mithraism taught a seven-fold division of the soul to which corresponded seven creations. When the soul first descends

[1] King: op. cit.
[2] Cf. Bigg: op. cit.

from the height of heaven to earth, it passes through the gates of the planetary spheres. By this means the soul acquires at birth the dispositions and qualities peculiar to each of these stars. After death it returns to its celestial home by the same path. Then, as it traverses the zones of the sky, it divests itself of the passions and faculties it has acquired on earth. To the Moon (which, it will be remembered, collects and purifies the seed of the Bull) it surrenders its vital energy; to Mercury, its cupidity; to Venus, its amorous desires; to the Sun (which, significantly, is in the fourth Heaven—the Paradise of Christian terminology) its intellectual capacity; to Mars, its warlike proclivities; to Jupiter, its ambition; to Saturn, its sloth. 'It is naked, disencumbered of all sensibility when it reaches the eighth heaven, there to enjoy as a sublime essence, in the eternal light where live the gods, bliss without end.'[1]

Mithra himself, as protector of truth, presided over the judgement of the soul; as mediator, he served as the guide of the faithful in their ascent through the seven heavens (for only his initiates knew the appropriate formula which would appease the angel guarding the gate of each planet); as their celestial father, he received them in his house of many mansions, as children who had returned from a distant voyage. So, in Mithraic temples are to be found seven ladders, the ascent of which by the initiate typified his passage to Heaven —a symbolism which persisted in such late orthodox Christian mysticism as, for example, the thirteenth century 'Seven steps of the Spiritual Ladder of Love', which defined the technique of union with the Deity.

As Mithraism developed, the doctrine of the inconclusive strife between good and evil was modified. The religion did not, indeed, abandon dualism; nor did it, like its Christian rival, teach that the victory over sin and death had, once for all, occurred. But it foreshadowed a time when, after the scourges sent by Ahriman should have accomplished the destruction of the world, a marvellous Bull, analogous to the

[1] Cumont: *Astrology and Religion.*

Primal Bull, would again appear and Mithra would descend to earth and awaken all men to life.

At that day when, putting on their bodies that all may recognize each other, mortals should come out of their tombs, Mithra would separate the good from the bad. Then, in a supreme sacrifice, he would immolate the Divine Bull, would mingle its fat with the consecrated wine and would offer to the just the miraculous beverage which should make them immortal.[1] Jupiter-Ormuzd, yielding to the prayers of the blessed, would send from heaven fire to consume the wicked and, in the general conflagration, Ahriman himself would perish and the rejuvenated universe enjoy eternal happiness.

Fundamental though the difference between the Christian Gnostic and the Mithraic Initiate is, it is easy to see why the ordinary man, merely content to practise the outward observances of religion and with neither knowledge of nor desire for 'salvation-technique', should confuse the two. Also, and more important, there was a perpetual tendency for distinctions to be blurred within the two cults. The crucial point, of course, was the historicity of Jesus Christ and the admittedly mythological nature of Mithra. For the Gnostic, even at his most extreme, 'the True Gate is Jesus the Blessed'. 'Alien as Gnosticism is to Christianity, yet the Gnostics claimed to be Christian and claimed it with apparent justification inasmuch as they consciously connected salvation with the Person of Jesus Christ. . . . For Gnosticism took not only the *name* of its saviour from Christianity; it was convinced—in varying degrees in different Gnostic sects—that it represented genuine Christianity. Jesus Christ is the great turning-point of world history. He succeeded, where all His predecessors failed, in leading the souls imprisoned in matter up to their Divine origin. For the Gnostics He is therefore *Saviour* in an exclusive sense, and so they can lay claim to be reckoned as Christians.'[2]

---

[1] The cup in which this drink is offered becomes later, as we shall see, the Grail.

[2] Nygren: *Agape and Eros*, II. i (1938).

On the other hand, they did not—as far as can be ascertained—really consider Christ as Saviour in the full Christian sense—that is to say, that He *was* God and that He *had* on the Cross accomplished the final defeat of Evil. Rather He is the teacher and revealer of the secret Gnosis and the Forerunner on the Way of Salvation. And this conception could easily become implicitly, if not explicitly, indistinguishable from philosophical dualism and a rejection of historical particularity—in fact, Mithraism.

6. The Manichees

The situation, already sufficiently equivocal, became further complicated by Mani, an aristocratic Persian who began, as a young man of twenty-six, to proclaim his new religion in the year A.D. 242 in the streets and bazaars of Ctesiphon. 'Such was his success that within a century, in the midst of the decay of Graeco-Roman paganism and the public triumph of Christianity, it seemed to many observers doubtful whether Manichaeism would not overwhelm them both.'[1]

The teaching of Mani was that there were two eternal sources or principles, Light and Dark; that by a regrettable mixture of Dark and Light the visible universe has come into being; and that the aim of those who are the Children of Light is not the improvement of this world, which is impossible, but its gradual extinction by the separation of the Light particles from the Dark substance. Light and Dark, which are as eternal, separate and different as the Ormuzd and Ahriman of the original Zoroastrianism which is the basis of Mani's thought, have associated with them, on the one hand everything that is Good, orderly, peaceful, intelligent; on the other, all that is Bad, anarchic, turbulent, material. In the Realm of Light dwells the Father of Greatness, with his Light, his Power and his Wisdom, forming a Quaternity—the Four-Faced Father, which Manichees con-

[1] Burkitt: *The Religion of the Manichees* (1925).

verts to Catholicism had to abjure; in the contiguous Realm of Dark lurked the King of the Dark, with his restless and infernal brood.

Into the details of the Manichaean cosmogony, it is unnecessary to enter except to say that it contains all the elements of the usual pattern which has already appeared in a simpler form in the original Zoroastrianism. Mani, however, was also concerned to reconcile these with Christianity. All his letters began with 'Mani, the apostle of Jesus Christ' and 'Jesus' meant to the Manichees not only the revealed and visible Light and the doctrine of the true destiny of man, but also Man's life and salvation through Divine suffering. They believed that they had in their religion the true 'word of the Cross'. But in exactly what sense they considered Him so, it is as difficult to determine as it is to know the true Gnostic belief.

In one respect, at least, it introduced a new line of thought and shifted the battle-ground. So far the problem could be and had been considered in terms of 'God' and 'His Creatures'. The question was whether and how far Jesus—'the Jesus who appeared in Judaea'—could be reckoned as 'God' or as 'Creature'. But to Mani this question was meaningless. His two categories were 'Light' and 'Dark' and consequently a 'Creature'—Man—was not even a unit, much less an elemental unit. He was 'a particle of Light, enclosed in an alien and irredeemable envelope; there is no hope for Man, as such, for he is essentially a fortuitous conglomeration. The hope is that his "Light-particles"—roughly speaking very much what we mean by his "better self"—may escape from the dark prison-house of his body'.[1] In the same way 'God', as the Manichees understood the term, meant anything composed wholly of Light-substance.[2] With these ideas as terms

[1] Burkitt: op. cit.

[2] Cf.: 'This then is the message which we have heard of him (Jesus, the Logos) and declare unto you, that God is light and in Him is no darkness at all.' 1 John i, 5.

of reference, the 'Jesus', the true Light honoured by Mani could obviously have been human in appearance only. The Manichees, no less than the majority of Gnostics, did not believe that He was really born or really crucified—but only so in appearance.

The practical organization of the Manichees also recalls that of the Gnostics. They were divided into the 'Elect' and the 'Hearers'. The 'Elect' alone was the true Manichee, on whom the command not to procreate life was binding. Besides marriage, they also renounced property and were supposed to live a wandering life. The 'Hearer', however, was allowed to marry and have property in the world, though his main duty was to care for the 'Elect'.

7. The Albigenses, or Cathars

Manichaeism, spreading westwards, was thus a corpus of ideas well fitted to assimilate the theories already prevalent in Mithraism and Gnosticism and, entering into their inheritance, to keep the old belief alive until in the Albigenses, the Catharist church of eleventh-century Europe, they appeared in another form.

The thread runs, as we saw in the introductory summary, by way of the Paulicians or 'Bulgars' of the seventh to the tenth centuries. 'In the Paulician faith, we find two co-equal principles, God and Satan, of whom the former created the invisible, spiritual and eternal universe; the latter the material and temporal, which he governs. Satan is the Jehovah of the Old Testament; the prophets and the patriarchs are robbers and, consequently, all scripture anterior to the Gospels is to be rejected. The New Testament, however, is Holy Writ, but Christ was not a man, but a phantasm—the Son of God who appeared to be born of the Virgin Mary and came from Heaven to overthrow the worship of Satan.'[1]

The identity of these beliefs with those we have been con-

[1] H. C. Lea: *A History of the Inquisition in the Middle Ages* (1906).

sidering is sufficiently obvious and their survival in the Albigenses will be apparent by a simple statement of some of the tenets of the Catharist church.

This 'Church of Love' taught that God is Love, but the world is evil. Therefore God cannot be the author of the world, with its darkness and sin. A first creation of the world was being carried out by God when, while it was still unfinished, it was interrupted by the rebel Angel—Satan or the Demiurge —who then completed it. Man is a fallen angel, imprisoned in matter and subject to the laws of the body—in particular the most oppressive of these, the law of procreation. But the Son of God came to show the way back to the Light, though the Christ was not incarnated, but only put on the appearance of a man.

The Cathars were composed of two groups—the 'Perfect' and the 'Believers'. The latter alone were allowed to go on living in the world and were not bound to comply with all the precepts of the esoteric morality of the 'Perfect'—bodily mortification, contempt for creation and the severing of 'worldly ties'.

The Cathars acknowledged only one sacrament—baptism by the consolatory Holy Ghost in the Kiss of Peace bestowed by the priest, after the reading of the Prologue to the Gospel of St. John, on the new brother at the initiation ceremony of a 'Perfect'. Before receiving this Kiss of Peace, the neophyte was required to undertake, among other things, that he would devote himself to God and His Gospel, that he would never be untruthful, that he would avoid touching his wife, if he were married, and that he would keep his faith a secret.[1]

'A further irrefragable evidence of the derivation of Catharism from Manichaeism is furnished by the sacred thread and garment which was worn by all the 'Perfect' among the Cathari. This custom is too peculiar to have had an indepen-

[1] The chief recent authorities for Catharism are Roche: *Le Catharisme* (1937), and Rahn: *Der Kreuzzug gegen den Graal* (1927). They have been used by Denis de Rougemont in *Passion and Society* (1940) whose epitome I have followed here; but the matter is treated in full in Part III.

dent origin and is manifestly the Mazdaean "kosti" and "saddarah", the sacred thread and shirt, the wearing of which was essential to all "believers". . . . Among the Cathari the wearer of the thread and vestment was what was known among the inquisitors as "haereticus indutus" or "vestitius" —initiated into all the mysteries of heresy.'[1]

Among the Cathars, it seems that the 'Perfect' only were so distinguished, since the thread was bestowed after the giving of the Kiss of Peace on initiation; but it is possible that the 'Believers' also had some distinctive token.

The most famous section of these 'Believers' were the Troubadours which meant (as is more obvious in the Old French form 'trouvère') a finder or discoverer. They were the Provençal founders of lyric poetry who, from the end of the eleventh to the middle of the thirteenth century, wandered in pairs over the countryside, singing the enigmatic songs in which the doctrines of the sect were enshrined. Their poetry is granted, even by strictly literary critics who are in no way concerned with—or, apparently, even aware of—the true nature of what they occasionally stigmatize as 'nonsense verse', to be derived from the popular folk poetry which was sung on May day, to the accompaniment of a ritual dance, in celebration of the rebirth of Nature.

Much of the Catharist belief is necessarily impossible to reconstruct, but it seems that it may have taken from its antecedents something of the significance of forms and numbers, especially the number four, recalling both the Manichaean Father and the Mithraic Fourth House of the Sun.

A curious piece of evidence may still be examined. In the finest known manuscript of the Apocalypse (in the library of Trinity College, Cambridge), the work of a French illuminator of the thirteenth century, the most elaborate of all its decorations is the heading to Chapter XIV, which fills half a page. It shows the Lamb, standing on Mount Zion, surrounded by the Elect. Above is the Godhead, typified by an

---

[1] Lea: op. cit.

immense golden *quatrefoil*, in which is seen an empty throne covered with a cloth crossed by diagonal blue lines. In each diamond so formed is painted in red a circle containing a point.

The comment that 'this geometrical expression of the idea of Deity, so opposed to the characteristic anthropomorphism of regular Gothic art, may perhaps have been inspired by the Manichaeist spirit that still actuated Southern France' receives confirmation from the subject itself.

The whole of the Apocalypse is unintelligible without some knowledge of the beliefs we have been discussing; but the particular passage which the scene represents is unquestioningly and uncompromisingly Gnostic. Archdeacon Charles, in his great commentary on the Book, clearly recognizes the heretical character of the opening of Revelation xiv: 'And I looked, and lo, a Lamb stood on the mount Sion and with him an hundred and forty-four thousand, having his Father's name written in their foreheads. . . . And they sung as it were a new song before the throne, and before the four beasts and the elders; and no man could learn that song but the hundred and forty-four thousand which were redeemed from the earth. These are they which are not defiled with women; for they are virgins. These are they which follow the Lamb whithersoever he goeth. These were redeemed from among men, being the first-fruits unto God and to the Lamb.'

Dr. Charles attributes this last, and crucial, verse to an editor whom he designates as 'an arch-heretic of the first century though probably an unconscious one' who 'introduces into Christianity ideas which had their origin in Pagan faiths of unquestionable impurity'. It is not quite as simple as that, but the commentator is undoubtedly right in seeing—what cannot escape even the casual reader—that according to this teaching 'marriage is a pollution' and 'neither St. Peter nor any other married apostle nor any woman whatever would be allowed to follow the Lamb on Mount Sion'.

Before proceeding, however, to the question of the relationship of orthodox Christianity to the deviations from it, it might be well to consider the career and metamorphoses of Mithra in the north of the Continent and especially in this country.

8. *Mithra in Britain*

Though our present state of knowledge leaves much still obscure about Druidism, we know certainly from ancient historians that Britain was reputed to be its fountain head and that its priests in Gaul were famous as philosophers as early as the beginning of the second century before Christ. We know also, though so much pre-history is uncertain, that in 500 B.C. when Cyrus the Persian was ruling his empire, Gaul was already being civilized by the Greek influence radiating from the Greek colony of Massilia (Marseilles) founded in 600 B.C. According to Justinus 'such a high degree of civilization was attained that it seemed as though it was not Greece that had come to Gaul, but that Gaul had been transplanted into Greece'.[1]

When the Carthaginians closed the straits of Gibraltar to the Greek merchants, in the sixth century B.C., the supply of tin was cut off, and the Cornish tin trade (by way of Cornish ports and overland through Gaulish trade routes) entered into its era of greatest prosperity. Not until Caesar's conquest of the Veneti, in the middle of the last century B.C., did the international character of this trade decline—and thus for practically the whole of five hundred years of the pre-Christian era which we have been discussing, there was a regular channel for the interchange of ideas between this country, the Mediterranean and the East.[2]

It may be that, by the time Roman writers came into contact with Druidism it was already in its decadence. Of its

[1] Just. XLIII, 4, quoted in T. D. Kendrick: *The Druids* (1927).

[2] This fact should be borne in mind when considering, for example, the 'legend' that Joseph of Arimathea visited tin-mines which he owned in Cornwall. It would have been as normal and natural a proceeding as it would be to-day for a London business man to fly to New York.

teachings we know, from Caesar,[1] that it stressed the immortality of the soul and, from Pliny, that the subjects of study were literally those of the Magian Gnosis.[2] It expressly taught the eternal existence and antagonism of the Two Principles, the final triumph of the Good and the Renovation of all things. The Druids were versed in astrology and paid particular veneration to the Moon and the Sun. Their central ritual seems to have been the sacrificial killing of a white bull under the sacred oak after the cutting of the mistletoe. There were, apparently, two main divisions, the full initiates, who were the Priests, and the 'Bards'; and under the rule of the priestly caste, the country enjoyed a very high degree of civilization centuries before Caesar's landing.

This current Druidism explains the ease and rapidity with which the Mithraism introduced by the Roman legions swept Britain. All the stations on the Wall appear to have had a Mithraic temple, where the Prefect of the place furnished an example of devotion to his subordinates. At York, the Mithraic altar stood in Micklegate Hill and contained the usual sculpture of the Bull-sacrifice. In London the rites were celebrated in a cave by the River Walbrook, near Bond Court. The present Abbey at St. Albans is on the site of a Mithraeum; and Colchester, Caerleon, Chester and other centres were devoted to the worship.

How far Druidism and Mithraism existed side by side in Britain, or how far they were synthesized, it is impossible to tell; but neither their inner philosophy nor their outward ritual presented any difficulties to an almost complete fusion. We know at least that in Gaul, the Arch-Druid Chyndonax placed his ashes, in his burial inscription, under the protection of Mithra. The tomb (which was discovered in 1598) proclaims: 'In this tomb in the sacred wood of the god Mithra is contained the body of the High Priest Chyndonax. May the

---

[1] De Bell. Gall. VI, 13 *et seq.*

[2] *Nat. Hist.*, XXX, 4. (See also Plutarch's *Doctrine of the Sons of Saturn*).

gods guard my ashes from all harm.'[1] And, in remote places, the rites—either Druidic, Mithraic or a synthesis of the two—lingered on for centuries, as we may see from the fact that on 5th September 1656 the Presbytery of Applecross summoned numerous parishioners to appear before them on the charge of sacrificing bulls at the 'dyke' or enclosure at Innis Maree, Ross-shire, on a date in August.[2]

The conflict of the Old Religion with Christianity begun in the last days of the Roman occupation was continued by Druidism in the period between the withdrawal of the Roman legions at the beginning of the fifth century and the consolidation of the Anglo-Saxon conquest at the beginning of the sixth. From the various waves of invaders, paganism was reinforced by a version of the old faith, at once more crude and more vital than Druidism in its sophisticated decadence. But Mithra, even when the whole land became officially Christian, was not defeated. If in the South, he was to be traced in the songs of the Troubadours, in the North he hid himself in the legend of the Holy Grail.

Dr. J. L. Weston has established that the original stories which developed into the Arthurian romance—those of *Perceval* and *Gawain*—had their rise in precisely those regions where Mithraic remains are known to exist. She has identified the original author, Bleheris, with Bledri, the son of that Cadivor, who entertained William the Conqueror on his visit to Wales and who died in the year that William Rufus ascended the throne. Her contention (which has not been successfully challenged) is that the Grail story is not a product of imagination, but the record, more or less distorted, 'of an ancient ritual, having for its ultimate object the initiation into the secret of the sources of Life, physical and spiritual. . . . In its esoteric "Mystery" form it was freely utilized for the imparting of high spiritual teaching concern-

---

[1] A picture of the urn appears in Spence: *Magic Arts in Ancient Britain* (1945).

[2] Spence: 'Survivals of Cult Practice' (*Hibbert Journal*, July 1941).

ing the relation of Man to the Divine Source of his being and the possibility of a sensible union between Man and God. The recognition of the cosmic activities of the Logos appears to have been a characteristic feature of this teaching. . . . When the struggle between Mithraism and Christianity ended in the definite triumph of the latter, the higher ritual still survived and was celebrated in sites removed from the centres of population—in caves and mountain fastnesses; in islands and on desolate sea-coasts.

'The earliest version of the Grail story, represented by our Bleheris form, relates the visit of a wandering knight to one of these hidden temples, his successful passing of the test into the lower grade of Life initiation; his failure to attain the highest degree. . . . The *mise-en-scène* of the story, the nomenclature, the march of incident, the character of the tests correspond to what we know from independent sources of this Nature Ritual.'[1]

In the Mithraic ritual proper there were seven grades. These, in ascending order of importance, were the Soldier, the Raven, the Persian, the Lion, the Hidden One, the Sun and the Father. They could be bestowed only by the Pater Patrum. After the initiate had passed various trials of fortitude, subdued his passions and made an act of renunciation, he was given the 'Crown of Mithra' ('Mithra is my Crown') and 'sealed' on the forehead as a 'tried soldier of Mithra'. He was then baptized to the remission of sins and allowed to make a partial act of communion. Full communion was allowed only to Lions and before attaining this grade, he had to suffer 'death'—symbolic murder at the hands of the Pater Patrum.[2]

'The mythical explanation of this act would run: "Mithra produced vegetable and animal life by the slaughter of the

[1] J. L. Weston: *From Ritual to Romance* (1922). It may also be remarked that G. F. Rowbotham in *Troubadours and Courts of Love* (1895) takes for granted that the Arthurian cycle is the work of English troubadours.

[2] W. J. Phythian-Adams: *Mithraism* (1915).

Bull; so also he produced human life by the murder of a (Primeval) man." And the mystical doctrine drawn from this creative act would be: "By suffering 'death' at the hands of the Pater Patrum, the initiate passes into true 'life'. . . ." Whatever we may think about the rite—the ritual murder— its existence cannot be gainsaid.'[1]

After 'death', honey instead of water became the baptismal agent and the Lion was presented with the consecrated wine which, in the Latin world, took the place of the sacred Haoma of the Persians.

At an initiation ceremony—or indeed at any service—the various grades wore the special costumes appropriate to them; and in the Mithraeum, at Ostia, there are seven semi-circles inscribed upon the pavement which suggests, according to Phythian-Adams that 'the Mithraic priests were in the habit of invoking the Planets from their special stations in the "cella" (aisle)', though it may also have some connection with the grades. In any case, it is probable that each grade was in some way connected with its special planet.

A full commentary on the relation of the Mithraic ritual to the Arthurian cycle would need the collaboration of scholars in different fields,[2] but the Grail as the life-giving cup which Mithra bestows on his initiates is obvious enough. It may be relevant to this ritual to cite the so-called 'Somerset Giants', which still awaits competent archaeological and anthropological attention. The Giants—or the Temple of the Stars—are the Signs of the Zodiac outlined in a circle ten miles in diameter near Glastonbury. Ten of the zodiacal signs, in the proper sequence, are distinguishable. 'If a wooden planisphere of the correct scale be placed over a map of the Giants and the stars of the signs be pricked through, these stars, in almost every instance, fall into corresponding

[1] Commodus profaned the mysteries by actually killing a would-be initiate.

[2] The association of the Raven with Arthur, for example, may be one of the connecting-links. See Lewis Spence: *The Magic Arts in Celtic Britain* (1945).

figures on the map. The exceptions fall in their vicinity. . . The Giants are formed by natural and artificial waterways, ancient tracks and hills which, with occasional old earthworks, model some of the figures in partial relief.'[1] Here, surely, may be the scene of initiation of which the ritual is preserved in the Arthurian cycle.

The Grail-cult proper was, of course, consistently opposed by the Church, which later, however, 'Christianized' the Grail as the Chalice of the Eucharist. This metamorphosis is easier to study, though it is outside the bounds of our inquiry; but the general question as to how far Christianity appropriated and absorbed the practices and symbolism of Mithraism —and, above all, in what sense the transformation was accepted by many apparently orthodox Christians—is eminently relevant.

But before this can be touched on, it will be necessary to trace the other trend of thought, through Egypt and Israel, which existed in the ancient world side by side with the dualism of which Mithra is the symbol.

[1] Harwood Steele in an article on 'The Somerset Giants' in *Country Life*, 11th January 1946. The article is illustrated by a map and aerial photographs reproduced from the Air View Supplement to *A Guide to Glastonbury's Temple of the Stars*, by K. E. Maltwood. With some of the text of the article, I find myself in disagreement, especially the suggestion that the date is about 3000 B.C. 500 B.C. would from 'internal' evidence be more likely. But the general thesis seems not only possible but extremely probable since, if the circle did not exist at that point, literary and theological evidence would lead one to postulate it.

Chapter IV

JEHOVAH AND JESUS

---

1. Palestine

The geographical position of Palestine has ensured its importance in world-history for thirty centuries. As it was the link between Europe, Asia and North Africa, whenever one of the great powers, in the first ages of world-imperialism, sought to reach the other, in peace or in war, the easiest route lay through Palestine. The possession of the fertile plain of Esdraelon, guarded by the mountains of Samaria, was indispensable to any would-be conqueror. In peace, all the great trade-routes crossed it. If Mesopotamia was the cradle of civilization, Palestine was the melting-pot of its races and religions. A thousand years before Christ—at the time of the establishment of the Davidic kingship—it was already an epitome of the world.

Its latest settlers, the Philistines, who gave their name to the land, were the remnants of one of the greatest civilizations of the ancient world—that centred in Crete, Asia Minor and the Greek mainland. The original settlers had been of Mesopotamian origin and the civilizations of Babylonia and Egypt were the background of 'Canaanitish' culture and belief. 'When the Hebrews came into contact with Canaanite culture, the processes of disintegration and degradation had, no doubt, been at work for centuries, but it is a legitimate inference from the general form and attributes which we find among the gods of the ancient East that very much the same pattern of daily offerings, Seasonal Festivals and private

58

rituals was going on in Canaan as in Mesopotamia from 2000 to 1000 B.C.'[1]

The evidence for this, which includes an examination of the Ras Shamra tablets, with their myths of Baal, as well as an understanding of certain passages of the Old Testament, need not be given in detail here; but it can be accepted that 'so far as the general situation is concerned we have reason to believe that both Egyptian and Babylonian influences were present in the patterns of temples, seals, representations of the gods and other cult accessories and that the main outlines of the Canaanite cult took their shape from this dominant Egyptian-Babylonian pattern.'[2]

During the whole period of Israelite history—that is to say, from the death of Moses and the entry of Joshua into the 'Promised Land' until the destruction of Jerusalem in A.D. 70— it is probable that, in one form or another, somewhere in the land, the cult persisted and that, until the Exile (597 B.C.), Sun-worship, under a very thin disguise, took place even in the Temple in Jerusalem itself. Apart from any other evidence for this, we have the perpetual fulminations of the Old Testament prophets.

What is important, however, is not the similarity of Israelitish worship to that of the rest of civilization, but its difference; not its affinity, but its repudiation and the emergence from the mass of influences and contradictions of the magnificent monotheism which was Israel's great gift to the world.

2. The One God

About the year 1375 B.C., in the Eighteenth Dynasty of Egypt when that country first became a world-power, there ascended the throne of the Pharaohs the young king Akhnaton, 'the first individual in history'. He was also known as 'the heretic King' on account of his efforts to found a new

---

[1] S. H. Hooke: 'The Ritual Pattern in Canaan' (in *Myth and Ritual*).
[2] Ibid.

religion which was, in effect, strict monotheism. To the current conceptions of the Sun God, which considered the Sun itself as the Deity, he opposed the notion of the sun as merely the symbol of a Divine Being whose energy was manifested in its rays. 'However evident the Heliopolitan origin of the new state-religion might be, it was not merely sun-worship; the word Aton was employed in the place of the old word for "god" (nuter) and the god is clearly distinguished from the material sun.'[1]

The inevitable controversy with the Egyptian priesthood which this policy precipitated resulted in the persecution by the King of the current religion, the closing of temples, the forbidding of services and the seizure of ecclesiastical property. He built a new capital named Akhetaton ('Horizon of Aton')—the modern Tell-el-Amarna; he made an inquiry into the wording of all existing monuments and ordered the effacement of any reference to 'gods' in the plural; he introduced a new representation of God—a round disc instead of the conventional pyramid and falcon; he denied belief in the whole theology of the Mysteries and their formulae—'Akhnaton flung all these formulas into the fire, spirits, monsters, demi-gods and Osiris himself with all his court were swept into the blaze and reduced to ashes'.[2]

After his death in 1358 there was an overwhelming and immediate reaction. His religion, which was confined to the small circle round him, had never been popular; and the people and Sun-Cult priests alike united in a fury of vengeance to wipe out his works and to proscribe his memory. But the influence of his monotheism and the School of Priests at On survived the catastrophe, even though Egypt as a whole returned thankfully to the worship of Isis and Osiris.

It is tempting to see in Moses one of Akhnaton's courtly followers who, after the king's death, kept alive his teaching among a band of captive Israelites whom, for this purpose,

[1] Breasted: *History of Egypt* (1906).
[2] Weigall: *Life and Times of Akhnaton* (1923).

he led out of Egypt to a new land.[1] But, in the present state of knowledge, the specific identification is impossible to make. For one thing, the date of the Exodus is still in scholarly dispute and shows no signs of being incontrovertibly settled. A tenable and generally accepted date, however, is some time between 1380 and 1300 B.C., in which case it would be reasonable to predicate some historical connection between Mosaic monotheism and the monotheistic episode in Egyptian history. At least the parallelism between Akhnaton's liturgy and Israel's worship of the One God is too patent to escape notice: 'In the two hymns to Aton, which have been preserved to us through the inscriptions in the rock tombs and were probably composed by him, he praises the sun as the creator and preserver of all living things in and outside Egypt with a fervour such as recurs many centuries after only in the psalms in honour of the Jewish God Yahweh.'[2] The Jewish religion is early differentiated from all others surrounding it by its silence about any life beyond the grave, which is intelligible if it is connected with the Aton cult's bitter attack on the realm and mysteries of Osiris. Circumcision is now known to have been an Egyptian, not a Jewish, custom in origin. That Moses should have made it the secret mark of a 'Holy People' is the more credible if he wished to make the Israelites in no way inferior to the Egyptians they were leaving and to distinguish them as the true worshippers of the One God.

The Mosaic religion, however, was not fixed in its final form by Jewish priests until the return from the Exile about 800 years after the Exodus; and it was not till then, after their contact with the fully developed Sun-worship in the Babylon of 500 B.C. with its essential dualism, that the uncompromising monotheism of their creed is apparent. The period between the establishment of the Davidic kingship (1000 B.C.) and the Exile can be understood only in the context of the culture pattern.

[1] See Freud's *Moses and Monotheism* (1939).
[2] Op. cit.

3. *Gerizim*

The Sacred Mountain of Israel was Mount Gerizim, the 'navel of the land' which stood in the centre of Palestine guarding the pass through the mountains to the fertile plains. In its shadow was the Sacred Well, known as 'Jacob's Well', in which the midsummer sun cast no shadows. By the well was the Sacred Oak and the reputed tomb of Joseph. All the early folk-stories led back to Gerizim. It was here that Abraham first entered the Promised Land and on the mountain that he prepared to sacrifice Isaac. Here he was met and blessed by Melchizedek, priest of 'the Most High God'. Here Jacob dreamt of the ladder which reached from earth to heaven. Here, at the time of the Israelitish entrance, Joshua set up his altar and made it the 'Mount of Blessing'. The Sacred Oak was the crowning-place of Abimelech and so potent were its associations that even after the establishment of the rival Temple on Mount Zion in Jerusalem, Rehoboam, Solomon's son, came here for coronation.

With the division of the country into the Northern and Southern Kingdoms—Israel and Judah—Gerizim in the North was gradually superseded by Zion in the South and the events which had been associated with the older appropriated—when they were not geographically impossible—by the devotees of the younger. Through the centuries the cleavage widened. 'The Samaritans'—Samaria, six miles from Gerizim, was the capital of the Northern Kingdom—remained, on the whole, the representatives of the Old Cult, however, superficially, they may at times have become Jahwehized.[1]

Their kingdom was the cosmopolitan centre where pagan influences were at their sharpest. By the great trade routes came in also the gods of the culture pattern—particularly Isis-Astarte—to reinforce the native worship of Baal who, whatever his metamorphoses, had never been expelled from his native mountain.

[1] It is this connotation of 'Samaritan' which must be borne in mind to understand the New Testament references to the 'Samaritans'.

When the Assyrians conquered Samaria (721 B.C.) Sargon re-colonized it with inhabitants of Babylon and its 'paganism' became in consequence even more marked; and though one of the native priests was eventually sent to teach the new inhabitants the nature of the 'God of the Land', it is improbable that that God was precisely the same as the God that was worshipped at Jerusalem.[1]

After the return from the Babylonian Captivity (535 B.C.) the breach between 'Jew' and 'Samaritan' became irreconcilable. The Jews refused to allow the Samaritans to help them rebuild the Temple of Jerusalem in spite of the Samaritans' protest: 'We seek your God as ye do and sacrifice unto Him'; and the Samaritans thereupon attempted to prevent the Temple being erected at Jerusalem at all.

Their own temple on Gerizim they eventually rebuilt by permission and authority of Alexander the Great and when the Jerusalem Temple was desecrated by Antiochus IV (168 B.C.) they asked that King's permission to dedicate their own temple to Zeus Hellenius.[2] This temple was destroyed as an avowedly pagan centre by John Hyrcanus in 109.

In apostolic times, Samaria was the home of the 'sorcerer' Simon 'the Magus', one of the most celebrated of all the Gnostics.[3]

The most important reference to Gerizim in the Bible, however, is that in which the Fourth Gospel represents Jesus Himself settling the rival claims of Gerizim and Zion. As He was sitting by the Sacred Well at noon-day, a Samaritan woman put the question to Him: 'Our fathers worshipped in this mountain; and ye say that in Jerusalem is the place where men ought to worship.' Jesus saith unto her: 'Woman, believe me, the hour cometh when ye shall neither in this mountain nor in Jerusalem worship the Father. Ye worship ye

[1] 1 Kings xvii.

[2] Josephus: Ant. XII, v.

[3] Acts viii—but this account should be compared with Simon's actual teaching—see chapter on 'Simonianism' in King's *Gnostics and their Remains*.

know not what: we know what we worship, for salvation is of the Jews. But the hour cometh and now is when the true worshippers shall worship the Father in spirit and in truth: for the Father seeketh such to worship him. God is a spirit; and they that worship him must worship him in spirit and in truth.'[1]

In what sense 'salvation was of the Jews' until in the person of Jesus Himself the separate significances of Gerizim and Zion were comprehended and abolished can be seen by considering what was the distinguishing mark of the Jerusalem cultus.

4. Jerusalem Renounces the Sun

It is important not to antedate the development of ideas in the worship at Mount Zion. Solomon's Temple was itself a Sun-Temple, built as the result of an eclipse of the sun on the site of the native Jebusite worship. 'The Jebusites were worshippers of the Sun-god; the Hebrews conquered them, but they did not evict the Sun from his sacred shrine on Mount Zion. It was the Jerusalemites' conception of Jahweh as Sun-god which long held the centre of the stage and only gradually retreated into the background.'[2] The pre-Israelite deity was known as El-Elyon (usually translated as the 'Most High God') and 'when we find that in the Davidic cultus, Jahweh plays the part of a Sun-god and is himself known as Elyon, it is only reasonable to assume that he has become the focus for ritual and mythology once associated with his traditional predecessor at Jerusalem'.[3]

Originally there could have been no thought of Zion superseding Gerizim as the national centre for 'the Temple was

[1] 5. John iv, 20–4.

[2] F. J. Hollis: 'The Sun Cult and the Temple at Jerusalem' (in *Myth and Ritual*). Ibid.

[3] A. R. Johnson: 'The Role of the King in the Jerusalem Cultus' (in *The Labyrinth*) (1935).

In these two essays the evidence for the statements above is given in detail.

certainly not built by Solomon for the purpose either of unifying the worship or of displacing other sanctuaries'. Its axis,
like that of Akhnaton's temple, was directed towards the east
—in this case towards the summit of the Mount of Olives
where the rising Sun-God revealed himself. The uninterrupted
line of vision between the Holy of Holies and the summit of
the Mount seems to have had a peculiar, if not magical,
significance and was connected with the ritual sacrifice of the
Red Heifer.

Although the prophets bore continuing witness to the
monotheistic—and eventually ethical—interpretation of the
worship, the Temple remained, in spite of spasmodic attempts at reform, the centre of a Sun-worship indistinguishable in the popular mind from the pagan cults. An epitome
of the situation as, on the authority of the Old Testament, it
appeared about 600 B.C., the eve of the Exile says that 'it
(The Temple) suggests a museum of curious and varied forms
of cult, collected from all the countries with which Judah had
come in contact. First we have mention of Baal and the
Asherah. These are probably relics of the old Canaanite worship. . . . The cult of the heavenly bodies, an astral worship,
had probably been introduced from Mesopotamia. . . . Another form of cultus from the same source was one which
involved sacramental fornication, including the homosexual
rites which were found in some parts of the ancient east. The
women of the Temple apparently had a special establishment in which they were employed in weaving and preparing
the sacred garments. Such an arrangement was to be found
in Babylonian temples. . . . One type of offering we cannot
trace at all. This was the dedication of chariots and horses to
the Sun-God. . . .[1] There seems to have been a special series
of stables to the west of the Temple assigned to this purpose.'[2]

But after the return from the Exile, there is a radical change
of which the open breach with the Samaritans is but one

[1] But may this not have been a remnant of Philistine worship?

[2] Oesterley and Robinson: *A History of Israel* (1932).

indication. The axis of the Temple was changed so as to disclaim once and for all any possible connection with the significance of the line of vision associated with the Mount of Olives. This change was emphasized by an alteration in the size and shape of the altar itself. And at the Feast of Tabernacles (that is to say the pre-eminently solar festival when Jahweh was worshipped as Creator) the Sun Cult was explicitly renounced. 'In Sukkah v, 4 we read "our fathers in this place stood with their backs to the Temple and they worshipped the sun towards the east, but we belong to the Lord and our eyes are directed to the Lord". We have here a clear and definite rejection of the Sun-cult. As there is no evidence that this cult survived to any large extent among the Hebrews after the Exile, it is to be presumed that the words quoted above, though late in themselves, refer to a change which took place, at latest, soon after the Exile.'[1]

The contact with the Mithraic and astrological system in Babylon had done its work. It had provoked among the 'Chosen Remnant' a lasting and militant reaction. The situation, in spite of the differences in time, circumstance and ethical implications, was parallel with the revolt of Akhnaton against the priests of Osiris. The One God, Lord of Heaven and Earth, had still His champions; and belief in the equality in power of Good and Evil was opposed by an assertion of the triumph of Righteousness. Zion and Gerizim went their separate ways and 'salvation was of the Jews'.

5. The Figure of Wisdom

No sooner had the Jews attained to a monotheistic belief— at the beginning of the fourth century B.C.—than it was again threatened by the power of the Mother-Goddess. The conquests of Alexander the Great made Judea a tributary of the Ptolemaic Empire, which was dominated by the Isis-cult. Though Isis inevitably retained her original attributes as

[1] Hollis: op. cit.

sorrowing wife and mother, the emphasis had by now shifted from the early simple identification with the Earth and Nature to 'the divine agent who created and sustained the universe and the teacher who had revealed to mankind the principles of morality and the laws and arts of civilization'.[1]

It was to counter the danger of a relapse into a worship of her, that the Jewish 'Wisdom literature' of the third century arose. 'The personified Wisdom is a female figure definitely on the divine side of the gulf which separates God from man. . . . Wisdom appears as the source of good counsel, strength and justice, through whom kings reign and do justice, and from whom all prosperity is derived. But she is more than this, for she is the first of God's creatures made by Him before He created the universe, yet delighting to dwell among the sons of men. . . . She remains the delight and darling of God, just as the Isis of the aretology is the eldest daughter of Cronos; and in some sense a link between God and man, as Isis in the aretology is the real intermediary between the gods and the world of men, for it is through her that man has learnt the knowledge of the gods and the method of serving them.'[2]

Since the classical references to Wisdom are so accessible (*Proverbs* in the Old Testament and *Wisdom* and *Ecclesiasticus* in the Apocrypha), elaborate comment is unnecessary here, though a quotation from one of her panegyrics on herself (Ecclesiasticus xxiv) may serve to show simply her nature and her original connection with the Mother-Goddess.

'I came out of the mouth of the Most High and covered the earth as a mist. I dwelt in high places and my throne is in a cloudy pillar. I alone compassed the circuit of heaven and walked in the bottom of the deep. In the waves of the sea and in all the earth and in every people and nation I got a possession. With all these I sought rest: and in whose inheritance shall I abide? So the Creator of all things gave me a command-

[1] W. L. Knox: *St. Paul and the Church of the Gentiles.*
[2] Ibid.

67

ment, and he that made me caused my tabernacle to rest and said, Let thy dwelling be in Jacob and thine inheritance in Israel. He created me from the beginning before the world and I shall never fail. In the holy tabernacle I served before him; and so was I established in Zion. Likewise in the beloved city he gave me rest and in Jerusalem was my power. And I took root in an honourable people, even in the portion of the Lord's inheritance I was exalted like a cedar in Libanus and as a cypress tree upon the mountains of Hermon. I was exalted like a palm-tree in En-gaddi and as a rose-plant in Jericho, as a fair olive-tree in a pleasant field, and grew up as a plane-tree by the water. I gave a sweet smell like cinnamon and aspalathus, and I yielded a pleasant odour like the best myrrh, as galbanum and onyx and sweet storax and as the fume of frankincense[1] in the tabernacle. As the turpentine tree I stretched out my branches, and my branches are the branches of honour and grace. As the vine brought I forth pleasant savour and my flowers are the fruit of honour and riches. I am the mother of fair love and fear and knowledge and holy hope: I therefore being eternal am given to all my children who are chosen of him. Come unto me, all ye that be desirous of me, and fill yourselves with my fruits. For my memorial is sweeter than honey and mine inheritance than the honeycomb. They that eat of me shall yet be hungry, and they that drink me shall yet be thirsty. He that obeyeth me shall never be confounded and they that work by me shall not do amiss.'

'There can be little doubt', writes Father Wilfrid Knox, 'as to the original of this highly coloured portrait. The lady who dwells in the city of Jerusalem and in its Temple, who is also to be compared to all the forest trees of Hermon and the luxuriant verdure of the Jordan valley, is the great Syrian goddess Astarte, at once the goddess of great cities and the mother manifested in the fertility of nature. The search for "rest" throughout the universe seems at first sight inappropri-

[1] The four ingredients of Jewish incense, cf. p. 33.

ate for Astarte as against Isis. But the two goddesses had been practically merged into one another for centuries before this and the particular feature of the quest of Isis had been adopted on behalf of Astarte. The change in the portrait appears to represent Isis in the character of Astarte or Astarte in the character of Isis, the ambiguous figure that appears on the coins of Antiochus Epiphanes.'[1]

The subsequent history in the Christian Church of this panegyric on Wisdom and its corresponding passage in Proverbs—the verses in the eighth chapter announcing: 'The Lord possessed me in the beginning of his way, before his works of old. I was set up from everlasting from the beginning or ever the earth was'—is not without significance for our general thesis. The latter was chosen as the Lesson for the Mass for the Immaculate Conception of the Blessed Virgin Mary—a feast observed in the East from about the eighth century and in England from the eleventh; the former provided the Lesson for the Mass of the Assumption of the Blessed Virgin Mary, which was observed generally from the fifth.

Though the doctrine of the Immaculate Conception, understood theologically, leaves Our Lady her creaturehood, there can be little doubt that, in the popular mind, it tends to raise her to the status of a quasi-divine being; and the opposition of such churchmen as St. Bernard and St. Thomas Aquinas to the dogma reflects the fear of their age that the Mother-Goddess might creep back under cover of orthodoxy. The fact that the Church did not proclaim belief in the Immaculate Conception *de fide* until the nineteenth century re-enforces this view, for by that time the force of the original associations was spent. The laity, hearing the Lessons to-day, would certainly not find in them the implications which would be patent to priests and scholars of the early medieval period. But when Becket, dying, commended himself to 'St. Mary', the invocation even supposing him to be orthodox[2] can hardly

[1] Op. cit.
[2] For the Cathar interpretation of 'St. Mary', see p. 144, n. 2.

69

be equated with a simple modern devotion to the Maid of Nazareth or the sorrowful Mother on Calvary.

Even in the centuries immediately before the birth of Christ, the sex and status of Wisdom presented difficulties to strict Jewish monotheism. With her metamorphosis and modifications we are not here concerned; but her final resting-place has relevance. She became merged in the Logos. 'In himself, the Logos is merely a substitute for Wisdom' as 'Wisdom herself had been transformed from her original character of Isis into the divine reason immanent in the Cosmos'. And 'the real effect of the introduction of the Logos was to make the divine Wisdom unnecessary; the fact that Logos is masculine made it a convenient substitute for the awkward feminine figure'.[1]

6. The Fulfilment of the Gentiles

In the person of Jesus, the varying streams of interpretation met. On His life and death all the roads converged. He was the fulfilment not only of Zion and Gerizim, but of the Logos, a world-idea. He abolished the rival Temples, because He Himself was the true Temple and brought metaphysics down to earth, because He was the Eternal Word and the pre-existing Wisdom.

His fulfilment of Jewish thought and prophecy has been the commonplace of all Biblical interpretation from the time of the Gospel according to St. Matthew (where it becomes slightly monotonous) until the present day. But it is only within the last eighty years, with the rise of anthropological study, that His relationship to Gentile belief—to Gerizim—has been adequately stressed. And this new knowledge has led to a readjustment of thought on at least one important point. The relationship was a *contemporary* relationship. Galilee 'of the Gentiles' was nearer to Gerizim than to Zion.

It is right that, in the story of the Passion, we should be-

[1] Knox: op. cit.

come conscious, as Archbishop Söderblom says, 'how strangely Christ fulfils even the idolatrous rites of weeping for Tammuz. . . and how the Roman soldiers had a dim sense of an inner meaning when they arrayed Pilate's prisoner as King of the May Revels, with purple robe and crown'. But it is even more essential to remember the significance of this to the people who actually saw it.

The remark of the bystander at the Cross, hearing the cry 'Eloi, Eloi' was, in all probability (as the Old Latin MS. k. preserved it) 'Behold, he calleth on Helios'. No Jew would be likely to confuse 'Eloi' with 'Elias' nor any Gentile to know who Elias was. But for a Gentile to interpret the cry as an invocation to the Sun-God—more particularly as the sun was mysteriously eclipsed—would be a natural mistake.

Again, Christ's promise to the dying thief: 'To-day shalt thou be with me in Paradise' had a very different implication to the actual hearers from that which subsequent Christian piety attached to it—for 'Paradise' was no vague 'Heaven', but the Fourth Heaven, the Mithraic House of the Sun.

A clue to such contemporary ideas is afforded by the insistence of the Fourth Gospel that the robe of which Jesus was stripped was 'without seam'. Quite apart from the fact that this verse contains the one, solitary allusion to the word 'seam' in the entire Bible, the circumstance that the Synoptic Gospels know nothing of the seamless tunic suggests that the matter merits investigation. The reasons usually advanced— that it provided a reason for the soldiers' throwing lots; that it showed that the robe was of local Galilean make; that it was symbolic of the unity of the Church—hardly match the occasion. Its significance becomes plainer when it is remembered that the sacred robe of the Zoroastrians (which, as we saw, continued to be, with the sacred girdle, worn by the Manichees and the Albigensians) had specifically *not* to be made of one continuous piece. It was essential that it should be made of two pieces sewn together at the sides so that one seam was on the right hand and the other on the left. What the writer of the Fourth Gospel is concerned with is to make plain that the robe of Jesus was not the robe of a Sun-Cult initiate as—it may legitimately be inferred, considering the nature of the Gospel as a whole—the Gnostics were, at the time of his writing, already contending that it was.

The tendency to mythologize the Crucifixion was not a later, but a contemporary, development. As Professor Bailey has put it, 'whether it is thought to have been part of a deliberate divine purpose or not, there was undoubtedly in the pagan world a "Praeparatio Evangeli", nor could the gospel have won its way if it had not found an echo in the religious searchings and even the religious beliefs of the time'.[1] And modernity has too often lost the sense of what the early Christian teaching in fact was. The idea of the Slain and Resurrected God, however strange it might appear to the Jews of the first and the scientific pagans of the twentieth century, was perfectly familiar to the Gentiles and had been for at least four thousand years. What the Apostles taught was that the man Jesus, whom their hearers had actually spoken to, had died and risen again and thus patently fulfilled the accepted and world-old conditions of divinity. And the thing was not done in a corner. The opposition was (and is) divided into two parties—those who accepted the Resurrection but continued to regard Him as merely a myth, and those who denied the Resurrection and dismissed Him merely as a man.

After the close of God's life on earth the pathways which had led to Him seem to diverge again, and follow their own previous directions almost uninfluenced by the episode of the Incarnation. But, in reality it is not so. It is a very superficial and unscholarly judgement which sees in, for example, the similarity of Christianity and Mithraism as they confronted each other for their struggle for power in the fourth century merely a proof of the Mithraic influence on Christianity. The parallelism is also and equally evidence of the Christian influence on Mithraism—though the exact contribution of each

[1] Bailey: *Phases in the Religion of Ancient Rome* (1932).

to the common likeness cannot now be certainly determined.

Since it is not always realized, except by scholars, how close the resemblance was, it may be well to outline it by a detailed quotation. 'The struggle between the two rival religions was the more stubborn as their characters were the more alike. The adepts of both formed secret conventicles, closely united, the members of which gave themselves the name of 'Brothers'. The rites which they practised offered numerous analogies. The sectaries of the Persian god, like the Christians, purified themselves by baptism; received, by a species of confirmation, the power necessary to combat the spirits of evil; and expected from a Lord's Supper salvation of body and soul. Like the latter, they also held Sunday sacred and celebrated the birth of the Sun on the 25th of December, the same day on which Christmas has been celebrated, since the fourth century at least. They both preached a categorical system of ethics, regarded asceticism as meritorious, and counted among their principal virtues abstinence and continence, renunciation and self-control. Their conceptions of the world and the destiny of man were similar. They both admitted the existence of a Heaven inhabited by beatified ones, situate in the upper regions, and of a Hell, peopled by demons, situate in the bowels of the earth. They both placed a Flood at the beginning of history; they both assigned as the source of their traditions a primitive revelation; they both, finally, believed in the immortality of the soul, in a last judgement, and in a resurrection of the dead, consequent upon a final conflagration of the universe.

'The theology of the Mysteries made of Mithra a "mediator" equivalent to the Alexandrian Logos. Like him, Christ also was an intermediary between his celestial father and men, and like him he also was one of a trinity. These resemblances were certainly not the only ones that pagan exegesis established between the two religions and the figure of the tauroctonous god reluctantly immolating his victim that he might create and save the human race was certainly compared to the picture of the Redeemer sacrificing his own person for the salvation of the world.'[1]

Or again: 'It (Mithraism) contains in outward and visible form, the sacred "Rock", the Sign on the Brow, Communion of Bread and Cup; and on its inward and spiritual side the doctrine of Sin and Redemption, Sacramentary Grace and Salvation to Everlasting Life. Is it surprising that in face of this astonishing similarity Christian apologists denounced the Mysteries as a most crafty and insidious attack upon the Truth? . . . With the Mithraic mysteries, as perhaps with no other pagan cult, there was to be a war of extermination.'[2]

It is hardly surprising that 'the God from the Rock was denounced by the Christian writers as a blasphemous caricature of their "sacred and venerable" secret that there was but one "Rock hewn without hands", one "Living Stone" which was Christ Himself'.[2] But to many who imagine that the deeper implications of that old rivalry are dead it may indeed be a surprise to know that in G. A. Gaskell's *Dictionary of the Sacred Language of all Scriptures and Myths*, published in 1923, a nonchalant entry runs: 'Mithras, god of the Rock is the same as the "Rock which is Christ".' (1 Cor. x, 4).

It is, nevertheless, the difference that matters. The inferiority of Mithraism was, ultimately, at the central point of the Christian truth. In the place of the passion of the Son of God sacrificed on the cross, there was only a mythical and symbolic redemption. It was the historical clause in the Creed— 'suffered under Pontius Pilate'—that was the Christian battle-cry.

7. The Spirit

The question that remained to be answered by those who accepted in some sense or other the revelation of God in Jesus and the special efficacy of His death was, Where and how was His continuing presence to be found? Gerizim and

[1] Cumont: *Mysteries of Mithra.*
[2] Phythian-Adams, op. cit.

Zion had gone and to them there was no return. But what was the nature of the new pattern of which He was the centre? How was He to be worshipped 'in spirit and in truth'? What *was* the Spirit that should lead men into all truth?

Since the majority of mankind has not yet found an answer and as Christians themselves have continued in evident disagreement on the subject, the controversies and heresies and speculations of the first twelve centuries are not altogether surprising. And they centred round the essential point of the reality of the human experience and death of God the Son. It was the Cross which was 'to the Jews a stumbling-block and to the Greeks foolishness'. In the development of the culture pattern, whatever the theory, two elements had in practice been stressed. The dualists had emphasized the Divine Combat, the monotheists the Divine Triumph. The Cross brought back into its pivotal position the Divine Sacrifice. The sophisticated centuries were suddenly confronted with the primitive beginning of it all. The Cross was Omega as well as Alpha and the clue to Life was Death. The metaphysical speculations which centred round a humiliated but ultimately triumphant Mediator were interrupted by the historical spectacle of the Slain God Who yet was Man.

He was also, according to one line of interpretation which in the New Testament is associated with the name of 'John', the Spirit of Love.

Chapter V

THE NATURE OF LOVE

1. Platonic Love

At this point it is necessary, for a full understanding of the problem, to introduce a new series of ideas and to approach it from a different direction. This line of inquiry concerns the nature of Love.

The meaning of the term 'God', in a transcendent sense, can only be understood through the experience of love. More, it is by love alone that any comprehenson of 'transcendence' is possible. Every other emotion is centred in the subject. Fear and praise, loyalty and devotion to an ideal, are, in the last analysis, grounded in egoism and God is perpetually made in the image of man. The object, however theoretically differentiated, is a mere metamorphosis of the subject.

But, through love, an object altogether different from the subject is discovered. It is possible for the Lover to act not for his own but for the Beloved's benefit and to act thus even if it involves his own hurt. Thus, in this way and in no other, can he break through the baffling circle of his own egoism. And once the path is perceived and 'transcendence' experienced, in however momentary and slight a form, the idea of 'God' can be understood. But there is no other way to 'the Other'.

Love itself, however, can be self-centred. The love of parent for child and of man for woman cannot, in the nature of things, be free from the dominance of the ego in one form or another. And 'Love', in so far as it is confused and confounded with the gratification of Desire, is the most overwhelming of all egoisms.

THE NATURE OF LOVE

The nature of the selfless love which leads to the comprehension of God and its differentiation from the egocentric love which is of the earth earthy was defined once for all by Plato. But since, in the course of centuries, the popular meaning of 'Platonic love' has deviated from the original significance of the phrase, it may be advisable to recall Plato's own definition, expressed though it is in the terms of conventional Greek mythology.

'Since Venus is of two natures, Love also must be dual. The elder and motherless goddess is the daughter of Heaven, and we call her Heavenly Venus; and the younger is the daughter Jove and Dione, and we call her Venus of the People. Necessarily, then, the companion Love of the one must be fitly called Popular, and that of the other, Heavenly. . . . Now the Love associated with the Venus of the People is of a common nature and functions promiscuously. This love is worshipped by the lower types of men who not only love women and youths equally, but love their bodies more than their souls, and prefer the least intelligent among them. For they care only to satisfy their desires and are indifferent whether the manner of their satisfaction be foul or fair. For this love proceeds from the Goddess who is not only younger than the other, but has a nature composed of feminine as well as masculine elements. But the other Love is of the Heavenly Venus and is felt only for males. She is the elder also, and lust has no part in her; therefore those who are inspired by this love turn to men, and love the stronger by nature and the superior by intelligence.'[1]

The detailed analysis of this love in which 'lust has no part' is carried to unrivalled heights in the *Phaedrus* with its picture of the lovers who have conquered desire, so that 'the better part of their nature has succeeded in bringing both lover and beloved into a life of order and philosophy and established its own ascendancy. In bliss and harmony they live out their existence here, being masters of themselves and decorous

[1] Plato: *Symposium* (Birrell and Leslie's translation).

77

before the world, having enslaved that portion of the soul wherein vice is contained and liberated that where virtue dwells; and at last when they come to die, being winged and lightened, they have in one of their three truly Olympic combats achieved the prize, than which no greater good can either human prudence or godly madness bestow on man'.[1]

Even with the meaning of 'Platonic Love' unequivocally clear, it is perhaps inadvisable to use it, so confused have its associations become. 'No phrase in English performs thinner or thicker work. It is made synonymous with the affections of the unimpassioned and a metonym for the disaffection or distemper of the virile. It is lifted like a veil over the love of a Dante and a Beatrice; of a Petrarch and a Laura; or it is depressed like a cloak on the Cloaca Maxima. By the man in the street "Platonic Love" is taken to signify decease or disease in the working of the erotic passion; disease when it connects the bodies and not the souls of the same sex, decease when it connects the souls and not the bodies in contrary sexes. But for Plato what was the meaning of "Platonic Love"? . . . Suffice it to say that after planting his ladder in the depths and mounting upon the possible rungs Plato reaches his final definition of Love and Beauty, but only after attaining the height exalted by Holy Scripture as the love that "was wonderful, passing the love of women".'[2]

The Victorian euphemism 'romantic friendship' is as unsatisfactory as the modern uninhibited 'homosexuality', for the one suggests the absence of desire and the other the absence of restraint. Possibly 'Uranianism', though an awkward term, is as neutral an equivalent as can be found for Plato's 'Heavenly Love'—Venus Urania.

By the nature of things this love can have no complete fulfilment. Biologically, it is that barrenness which, if the race is to continue, must be perpetually opposed. But spiritually, because it is in a mystical sense the death of Eros ('my Eros

[1] Plato: *Phaedrus* (Wright's translation).

[2] Introduction to Birrell and Leslie's translation of the *Symposium*.

is crucified'), it is the principle from which all creativity springs. Plato's 'Heavenly Venus' and 'Earthly Venus' might be described as 'creative love' and 'biological love'. Each to itself is 'life' but to the other 'death'. Further, each on its own plane is true to the unifying principle of the cosmos that the price of 'life' is 'death'.

Though, in theory the principles can be discriminated, no such separation is possible in practice. As for civilization so for the individual the interplay of both is the condition of the 'fulness of life'. The creativity which springs from the union of souls of those of the same sex, uniting in sacrifice, and the creation accomplished by the mutual surrender of bodies between those of the opposite sex, are complementary as well as antagonistic. From Shakespeare's passion for 'Mr. W. H.' sprang certainly the Sonnets and probably most of the plays.[1] But Shakespeare was also a citizen who founded a family and knew as certainly as any other breadwinner the drudgery and self-denial which the fulfilment of biological duties entails.

In terms of this tension of the two loves, the whole story of man and civilization can be comprehended; but it is by way of Platonic Eros that the Spirit of Love, which is God, can be found.

2. The Conspiracy of Silence

To eptomize the argument which is developed in a later chapter,[2] this point of view may be described in the now conventional theological terms of Agape and Eros by saying that Agape is Slain and Resurrected Eros. But here, for the purposes of the historical quest, it is enough to see the two loves in terms of the 'creative-biological' division—Uranianism and 'normal' sexual love. As I have already said, each

---

[1] The homosexual relationship is, for example, the key to such plays as *The Merchant of Venice* and *Julius Caesar*: and one of the greatest modern productions of *Othello* made the motivation the love of Iago for Othello—which interpretation alone makes the action comprehensible.

[2] See Chapter XII.

regards itself as 'life' and the other as 'death', though they are not, in fact, mutually exclusive. Their confusion is indicative of a general chaos of thought on the subject, due, in great measure, to what can only be called a general conspiracy of silence—an automatic censorship which, in its irrationality, has its roots in instincts deeper than reason.

'Creative' love, which is both the means by which man can arrive at an understanding of God and the source of his own most profound expression of himself, is unequivocally recognized as the 'higher' love by those capable only of 'biological' love. But side by side, and sometimes inextricably woven, with it is that other love which is merely sterile and is as far below 'biological' love as 'biological' love is below 'creative'. And the instinct which leads the 'normal' man to reverence 'purity' leads him also to loathe 'perversion'. The difficulty is that, in practice, he is never quite sure which is which; and, as any age or movement which is Uranian is more likely to appear to him as 'perverted' than as 'pure' and as effeminately sterile than as creatively masculine, the natural 'biological' reaction is to oppose the whole movement in the name of 'morality'.

In point of fact, the great ages of European culture are distinguished by a prevailing Uranian temper—the Periclean age of Greece, the Augustan age of Rome, the 'first Renaissance', the Renaissance, the Elizabethan age in England, the age of Louis XIV in France. Individuals, no less than ages, exhibit the same characteristic, whether soldiers like Caesar, Eugene and Frederick the Great, religious geniuses like Augustine, Francis of Assisi and Cardinal Newman, painters like Michelangelo, Leonardo da Vinci and Reynolds, poets so different as Marlowe, Gray and Tennyson, musicians such as Chopin, Wagner and Tschaikowsky, masters of prose like Bacon, Montaigne and Proust.[1]

[1] I have taken these random names as being a selection of those about whom no serious dispute is likely. I am not concerned with the (I think, untenable) hypothesis which suggests that homosexuality is the 'stigmata of genius'.

Though this is perfectly well known to and allowed for by scholars, it is seldom recognized by the generality of men. The conspiracy of silence sees to that. But this silence is due to something more pertinent than 'prudery'. The 'biological' protest against Uranianism is inevitable if the race is to continue on the plane of procreation; the safeguarding of Uranianism is vital if civilization is to continue on any other plane. Both, therefore, connive in the silence. The 'normal' man has no wish to ascribe to the 'abnormal' man the kudos of creativity; nor has the 'abnormal' man any wish to provide a justification for the 'subnormal' man to attach himself to him and, by his association, to provide an intelligible 'moral' excuse for an attack from the 'normal'.

A simple example may make clearer the efficacy of the conspiracy. Two Victorian homosexual poems—homosexual both in the source of their inspiration and in their essential subject matter—are Tennyson's *In Memoriam* and Fitzgerald's *Rubaiyat of Omar Khayyám*. So successful has the (automatic) 'biological protest' been that it is unlikely that the majority of Victorian owners of leather-bound copies of these works were aware of the fact or would have been anything but horrified had they been.[1] Nor, of the thousands who have publicly yearned 'to meet their pilot face to face when they have crossed the bar' (and Tennyson's poem is included in *Hymns, Ancient and Modern*), have the majority probably been aware that the 'pilot' is not God but Arthur Hallam. When it is remembered that this process of what may be termed the 'automatic bowdlerization of ideas' is consistently and potently at work in the interpretation of history—and religion—some idea may be gained of the difficulty of correctly assessing the motives and the movements of the past.

But it is against this background that the whole matter of

[1] Though *The Times* rebuked the language of *In Memoriam* as unfitted for any but amatory tenderness and Tennyson mentioned "the number of shameful letters of abuse he had received about it."

dualism, gnosticism, heresy and witchcraft must be placed if it is to be seen in proper perspective. When, as in the thirteenth century, the mob rose against the 'heretics', it was not a commendable manifestation of the innate piety of the common people in the 'Ages of Faith'. It was the natural protest of the normal citizen against a prevalent and prolonged fashion of what he assumed (whether correctly or not) to be sodomy. The Inquisition was established to safeguard individuals from reckless accusations and mob-violence and was a move not in the direction of fanatical persecution but of discriminating sanity. For the Church was more aware than the State of the necessity of Uranianism—which, in fact, underlay her own monasticism. In the beginning, the Christians had been enthusiastically persecuted because of their 'life denying' proclivities; it was as 'haters of life' that the Roman populace refused to tolerate them. In later days the monasteries were to go down under the accusation that they were 'a second Sodom and Gomorrah'. And in the thirteenth century the populace would have been quite as scandalized by the erotic mysticism of St. Bernard if they could have understood it, as by the more obvious manifestations of 'heresy' they were engaged in suppressing.

3. Clues in History

It is neither possible nor desirable to pursue the subject into its many historical and psychological ramifications, but it is necessary to suggest the main avenues by which Uranianism was connected with the cult.

The first and most obvious was the principle of the dualist philosophy that Matter was evil; that man's first duty was to refrain from procreation; and that salvation was bound up with celibacy.

In so far as this was based on a proper understanding of the nature of the Heavenly Eros, its strength lay in the truth it contained. But it also provided a system of belief and practice congenial to those of 'abnormal' temperament, whom it inevitably attracted.

The second point of contact was that the Mysteries were, in the main, rigidly confined to men. The Orphic Mysteries in particular were so obviously homosexual that Orpheus, who met his death at the hands of infuriated women, is the legendary embodiment of perversion. And Mithraism became pre-eminently the religion of soldiers—of 'men without women'. Without entering into the psychology of the military life, it is at least relevant to mention the most famous military formation of the ancient world—the Sacred Band of Thebes. The numerous allusions to it in classical literature attest its influence and even to-day it is not forgotten, though it is usually referred to in such a non-committal phrase as 'the *élite* of the Greek army'. Its uniqueness as a fighting force lay in the fact that it was composed of pairs of lovers and 'a band cemented together by friendship founded upon love is never to be broken, and invincible; since the lovers, ashamed to be base in the sight of their beloved, and the beloved before their lovers, willingly rush into danger for the relief of one another. . . . It was never beaten till the battle at Chaeronea[1]; and when Philip after the fight took a view of the slain, and came to the place where the three hundred that fought his phalanx lay dead together, he wondered and, understanding that it was the Band of Lovers, he shed tears and said: "Perish any man who suspects that these men either did or suffered anything that was base" '.[2]

The principle of the Theban Band survived to become the basis of feudal 'chivalry'. It is conventionally assumed—as part of the conspiracy of silence—that the key to chivalry was the extravagant worship of Woman. The Knight fighting for his 'Lady Fair' is almost the stock synonym for romantic love between the sexes. But the truth is almost the exact opposite.

[1] 338 B.C. Philip is Philip of Macedon, father of Alexander the Great.
[2] Plutarch: *Life of Pelopidas.*

'Love, in our sense of the word', writes C. S. Lewis in *The Allegory of Love*, 'is as absent from the literature of the Dark Ages as from that of classical antiquity. . . . The deepest of worldly emotions in this period is the love of man for man, the mutual love of warriors who die together fighting against odds, and the affection between vassal and lord. We shall never understand this last if we think of it in the light of our own moderated and impersonal loyalties. We must think not of officers drinking the king's health; we must think rather of some small boy's feeling for some hero in the sixth form. . . . He loves and reverences only what he can touch and see; but he loves it with an intensity which our tradition is loth to allow except to sexual love. . . . These male affections—though wholly free from the taint that hangs about "friendship" in the ancient world—were themselves lover-like; in their intensity, their wilful exclusion of other values and their uncertainty, they provided an exercise of the spirit not wholly unlike that which later ages have found in "love". The fact is, of course, significant.'

It is even more significant when it is remembered that there is really no justification for differentiating, as Mr. Lewis does, between the medieval and the classical type of 'friendship'. There is just as much and just as little 'taint' about the love of the knights of Christendom as about the Theban Band. And in the Troubadours where 'chivalry' finds its literary expression the connection between Uranianism and the cult becomes unmistakably apparent.[1]

[1] Even if we did not know that the Troubadours were Cathars, the nature of their love is sufficiently obvious; nor, in order to understand that the expressed love for the 'lady' was not altogether what it might seem, do we need the evidence that a courtly knight often gave his lady the masculine title of 'mi dons' (mi dominus) and that Dante assigns to the sodomites' circle of Purgatory two of the Troubadours noted for the ardency with which they extolled the beauty of their ladies—Arnaut Daniel and Guido Guinicelli.

In a poem of women another famous Troubadour, Rambaut of Orange, says: 'I do not want to be put to trouble for the sake of women any more than if they were all my sisters; and so with women I am humble, obliging, frank and gentle, fond, respectful and faithful . . . I

It is a matter of history that the charges against the heretics (and witches) always did include that of 'unnatural vice' and there is no reason whatever to suppose that this was an accidental coincidence or a manufactured charge to discredit them. On the other hand, it must be remembered that the true doctrine of the higher or 'Heavenly' love, of the Crucified Eros, was usually the inner mystery of the same sects and that, because of its correspondence to ultimate psychological realities, it remained despite all persecution undestroyed and indestructible.

Also, in so far as it was the truth, it remained in orthodox Christianity. It is the undercurrent of St. Paul's attitude to love; it is obvious in the teaching of St. John, the Beloved of Jesus; and it became overstressed and extravagant in the Apocryphal books in which the early Christian Gnostics by their very explicitness reveal the tendency in orthodoxy which might otherwise be unnoticed.

In the Latin *Epistle of Titus*, for example, there is a passage which balances and emphasizes the description we have already noticed in the Apocalypse concerning the '144,000 virgins' who are the Elect. 'Receive therefore in thy heart', this passage runs, 'the admonition of the Blessed John who, when he was bidden to a marriage, came not save for the sake of chastity, and consider what he said: Little children, while your flesh is pure and ye have your body untouched and not destroyed . . . know ye more fully the mystery of the nuptial union; it is the experiment of the serpent, the ignorance of teaching, injury of the seed, the gift of death; (31 more clauses of abuse): the impediment which separateth from the Lord, love nothing except this ring, which is dear to me because it has been on a finger . . . But I am going too far. Stop, tongue; because to say too much is worse than mortal sin.'

As de Rougemont says: 'We have been too long supposing that "courtly love" was a mere idealization of the sexual instinct. At the same time it would be going too far to assert that the mystical ideal on which "courtly love" must have been founded was always and everywhere being invoked *or that in itself it could have only one meaning*. Nearly everywhere an emphasis on chastity is accompanied by lewd excess.'

the beginning of disobedience, the end of life, and death
itself.'

There could hardly be a more forcible example of the way
in which 'creative' love regards 'biological' love as 'death'.
And in the *Acts of John*, the Beloved is represented as thank-
ing Jesus for thrice having prevented him marrying and having 'kept me until this (last) hour for Thyself, untouched by
contact with a woman': and Jesus as answering: 'John, if
thou hadst not been mine, I could have suffered thee to
marry.'[1]

The *Acts of John* were, indeed, specifically rejected at the
second Council of Nicaea in 787 (that is to say, about the
time of the great wave of Manichaeism in its Paulician form),
but more relevant than the ultimate rejection is the circumstance that, for a period of time as long as that between the
murder of Thomas Becket and our own day, it was *possible*
to hold these views within the bounds of an—admittedly
tenuous—orthodoxy. And even to-day, the characteristic
symbol which first meets the eye in any Catholic Church—
the Rood, with the Crucified between the Beloved and the
Mother—has a significance which is not always understood.

But in the fourth century, negatively as a safeguard against
heretical eccentricities, positively as the orthodox affirmation of the Christian truth, Augustine gave his great definition of the Trinity in which the Father is the Lover, the Son
the Beloved and the Holy Spirit the Love subsisting between
them. Here is the God of Love; here human love becomes
veritably divine in so far as it is 'in the Spirit'; here is the
meaning of transcendence; and here the mystical interpretation of the Cross is comprehended in a doctrine whose apparent simplicity conceals illimitable depths.

It is in the figure of a cross that we can perhaps see it simply.
There is the horizontal division between Christian and pagan;
but there is also the vertical division which runs through both
Christian and pagan, connecting those who share 'creative'

[1] James: *Apocryphal New Testament.*

love. At the point of intersection, and there alone, is that Love which is the 'Spirit' that shall 'lead into all truth'.

The Church had thus a dual function to perform in relation to Uranianism. On the one hand She had to protect it in its purity because it concerned the mystery of Her own life; on the other hand She had to safeguard society against the effects of its misuse. She had to act both 'creatively' and 'biologically', for both functions were implicit in the Incarnation.

But outside Her own Divine synthesis at the heart of the Cross, there was another point where other roads met. There was the paganism of the Old Religion meeting the Gnostic deviations from the New. Here, too, were the mystery of sacrifice and the acknowledgment of the creative power of broken desire. It was near enough the truth to be something more than a caricature of it, for its roots were in man's earliest beliefs, and the philosophy and psychology underlying its development were similar to—and sometimes shared by— orthodoxy.

And in practice this led to a bewilderment in which contemporaries could hardly discern the truth or posterity discover that there were many strange truths to discern.

II
THE HISTORICAL
CIRCUMSTANCES

Chapter VI

THE ELEVENTH CENTURY BACKGROUND

1. The Witches

In the Christendom of the eleventh century, there were three main movements of unorthodoxy. They were all derived from dualism. Inside the Church there was the gnosticism of the various neo-Manichaean sects, pre-eminently the Cathars. Outside the Church there were the philosophic pagans, inheritors of Mithraism and (in Britain) Druidism. The literature of the one was to be found in the lyric songs of the Troubadours; that of the other in the Grail Romances—both of which were condemned by the Church. Both found their social expression in the idea of 'chivalry'—which Dr. Arnold assessed better than he knew when he wrote: 'I confess that if I were called upon to name what Spirit of Evil predominantly deserved the name of Antichrist, I should name the Spirit of Chivalry'.[1] Both were distinguished by a Uranian temper, as a logical expression of their belief in the evil of matter; and this temper, at its best, attained heights of asceticism and, at its worst, explored depths of 'perversion' unknown to orthodoxy.

The third movement was 'witchcraft' proper—the 'popular' religion which was in fact the old fertility-worship, demanding both the occasional blood-sacrifice and the more

---

[1] Arnold to Archdeacon Hare in 1829 (*Life and Correspondence*). The reason Arnold gives—that it fosters a sense of honour rather than a sense of duty—seems hardly adequate for such an indictment.

frequent orgiastic 'sympathetic magic' of promiscuous sexual intercourse. That this Dianic cult had also the common dualistic basis is easily seen from its 'myth': 'Diana was first created before all creation; in her were all things; out of herself, the first darkness, she divided herself; into darkness and light she was divided. Lucifer, her brother and her son and her other half was the light.'[1] Diana came to earth in the form of a cat and, in that form, won access to Lucifer (for, as the Darkness, she could never overtake the Light) whom she desired, but who did not desire her.

The rites of the Dianic cult took place in a forest at full moon and consisted of dances, fertility ritual and conjurations of meal, salt, honey and water—the ordinary 'country magics'. And it seems probable that certain features recalled the Primal Bull of Mithraism and Druidism.

In the earliest ecclesiastical law of England, the *Liber Poenitentialis*, of Theodore, Archbishop of Canterbury (668–90), one section is occupied with this Old Religion and its rites.[2] It provides penances for 'not only celebrating feasts in the abominable places of the heathen and offering food there, but also consuming it: serving this hidden idolatry, having relinquished Christ: if anyone at the kalends of January goes about as a stag or a bull—that is, making himself into a wild animal and dressing in the skin of a herd animal, and putting on the heads of beasts; those who in such wise transform themselves into the appearance of a wild animal, penance for three years, because this is devilish'.

In the next century the *Confessionale and Poenitentiale of Ecgberht* (first Archbishop of York, 734–66) prohibits offerings to devils; witchcraft; auguries according to the methods of the heathen; vows paid, loosed or confirmed at wells, stones or trees; and the gathering of herbs with any incantation except Christian prayers.

A decree attributed to a General Council of Ancyra in the

[1] Leland: *Aradia or the Gospel of the Witches* (1899).
[2] Thorpe: *Monumenta Ecclesiastica* (1840), Vol. ii.

ninth century, refers to 'certain wicked women, reverting to Satan and seduced by the illusions and phantasms of demons, believe and profess that they ride at night with Diana on certain beasts, with an innumerable multitude of women, passing over immense distances, obeying her commands as mistress'.[1]

In the tenth century, the *Ecclesiastical Canons of King Edgar* (959) 'enjoin that every priest zealously promote Christianity and totally extinguish every heathenism; and forbid well-worshippings and the vain practices which are carried on with various spells and with "frith-splots", and with elders and also with various other trees, and with stones, and with many various delusions, with which men do much of what they should not. . . . And we enjoin that every Christian man zealously accustom his children to Christianity, and teach them the Paternoster and the Creed. And we enjoin that on feast days heathen songs and devil's games be abstained from'.[2]

And in the eleventh century, the *Laws of King Cnut* (1017–35) 'earnestly forbid every heathenism: heathenism is that men worship idols; that is, they worship heathen gods, and the sun or the moon, fire or rivers, water-wells or stones, or forest trees of any kind; or love witchcraft'.[3]

In endeavouring to assess the probable strength in Britain of the 'Craft of the Wise'—witchcraft—the background of centuries of Druidism amd Mithraism must not be forgotten. It may only have been in far and secret places that actual Mithraic initiation survived; and the Grail stories were not written to enshrine them till the twelfth century.[4] But the

---

[1] Lea: *History of the Inquisition* (1888), Vol. iii.

[2] Thorpe: op. cit.   [3] Thorpe: op. cit.

[4] It is worth perhaps quoting Dr. Weston's admission in *From Ritual to Romance*: 'Without entering into indiscreet details I may say that students of the Mysteries are well aware of the continued survival of this ritual under circumstances which correspond exactly with the indication of two of our Grail romances.' And again, 'The Grail Quest was actually possible then, it is actually possible to-day, for the indication of two of our romances as to the final location of the Grail is not imagination, but the record of actual fact.'

connection of the cult with the life of the ordinary man may be suggested by the following description: 'The gods were everywhere and they mingled in every act of life; the fire that cooked the food and warmed the bodies of the faithful, the water that allayed their thirst and cleansed their persons, the very air that they breathed and the light that illuminated their paths, were the objects of their adoration. Perhaps no other religion ever offered to its sectaries in a higher degree than Mithraism opportunities for prayer and motives for veneration. When the initiated betook himself in the evening to the sacred grotto concealed in the solitude of the forests, at every step new sensations awakened in his heart some mystical emotion. The stars that shone in the sky, the wind that whispered in the foliage, the spring or brook that babbled down the mountain-side, even the earth that he trod under his feet, were in his eyes divine, and all surrounding nature provoked in him a worshipful fear for the infinite forces that swayed the universe.'[1]

This might equally well have been written of the Dianic Cult, the 'witchcraft' which the Christian Church in England fought so persistently and eradicated so partially.[2] And, in looking back on the subject from the twentieth century, it must be borne in mind that the study of 'witchcraft' tends to centre in the period between the fourteenth and seventeenth centuries, when 'witchcraft' was a heresy, punishable by death. But during the whole of the period we are considering —that is to say, up till 1170—'witchcraft' was neither. It was a sin, because it was a superstition; and it merited penances of some severity; but it was neither a heresy nor a capital offence. It was not until the second half of the thirteenth century that it was officially pronounced heretical; and as late as 1282 the priest of Inverkeithing—though 'presented' before the bishop—was allowed to retain his benefice after leading a

[1] Cumont: *Mysteries of Mithra.*
[2] Cf. Modern pantheistic movements even within certain sections of the Church.

fertility dance at Easter round the phallic figure of a god.[1] And it is with no great sense of incongruity that we find that Thomas Becket, in 1170, the year of his death, neglected the dispatch of certain letters pertaining to his duties as Archbishop of Canterbury, because he was preoccupied in consulting the auguries and sooth-sayings of 'witches'.

It may be doubted whether the 'conversion' of England, which is associated with the landing of Augustine in 597, made very much impression on the common people. The hundred and eighty years between the withdrawal of the Roman legions and the arrival of Augustine had seen paganism reinforced by versions of the Old Religion brought over by the various waves of invaders; and 'in judging of the history of early Christianity in Britain it must always be remembered that the people who brought it in on the east coast were foreigners who never amalgamated with the natives. Augustine was Italian, and for more than a century no native Britons were advanced to high places in the Church. Theodore of Tarsus, with the aid of Hadrian, the negro, organized the Church in England in the seventh century; Italians and other aliens held the high offices. The Augustine mission and their successors concentrated on the rulers and through them forced their exotic religion on a stubborn and unwilling people. . . . No religion dies out with the dramatic suddenness claimed by the upholders of the Complete-Conversion theory. The constant influx of Pagans through several centuries more than counter-balanced the small number of immigrant Christians. The country, therefore, must have been Pagan, with Christian rulers and a Christian aristocracy.'[2]

A rough parallel is supplied by Spain under the Moslems, where the rulers were more obviously of one religion and the people of another, with the popular religion receiving reinforcements from abroad. There, however, the popular religion, aided by the civil power, drove out the superimposed

[1] *Chronicles of Lanercost*, ed. Stevenson.
[2] Murray: *The God of the Witches*.

cult. In the England of the eleventh century, the final conquest was by the Normans, whose rulers professed Christianity; but as the Norman people, like the English, were largely of the Old Religion, the Conquest did not alter materially the relative positions of the two creeds; and as it was preeminently the Normans, by their contacts in Sicily, who were instrumental in diffusing Gnostic and Manichaean elements in Christianity, the actual religious position became more, not less, confused with their advent.

In the seventy-five years before the Norman Conquest, the spread of the neo-Manichaean movement within the Church in France can be estimated by certain established facts. Gilbert of Aurillac—who was later to become Pope as Silvester II—was, on his election as Archbishop of Rheims in 991, obliged to make a profession of faith in which he explicitly declared his belief that Satan was wicked of free-will, that the Old and the New Testaments were of equal authority and that marriage was permissible. There was a Cathar centre in Champagne in 1000; in Orleans in 1017; in Liége in 1025; in Châlons in 1045; in Toulouse in 1056; in Béziers in 1062. When so much was open, when even priests in the highest places were suspected of secret allegiance to it, the actual range of the heresy is incalculable. And the dividing line between the Gnosticism within the Church and the frank paganism outside was even thinner than that between certain forms of orthodoxy and the purer forms of Gnosticism.

2. A Dance

To take one obvious example of the action and reaction of ancient fertility rites, sun symbolism, gnostic ideas and the Christian Gospel.

The dance, as an important part of the fertility rite, is probably the most primitive form of ritual; the ring-dance introduces as well the solar-pattern and syncretizes with the older phallic significance in taking place round a central stone, pillar or effigy of the god. The 'witch dance' during the Christian centuries seems to have consisted of a dance of the 'coven' (twelve initiates) round the 'Devil' (that is, the chief or 'god').

But the 'witch' ring-dance was much more than an inheritance of primitive superstition. In the hands of the Gnostics inheriting from the Magi, the symbolism had been refined into something altogether different. Not only had the circle a full zodiacal significance, not only was the circle and point a mathematical device of esoteric meaning, but the liturgical expression of the dance was connected with the heart of the Christian mystery.

In the *Acts of John*, to which reference has already been made—it was written about a century after the Crucifixion and was one of the five books subsequently formed into a *corpus* by the original Manichaeans and substituted by them for the canonical *Acts of the Apostles*—there occurs an account of the hymn sung by Jesus and His disciples in the Upper Room before going out to betrayal on the Mount of Olives.

John the Beloved is represented as saying: 'Now before He was taken by the lawless Jews, who also had their law from the lawless Serpent, He gathered us all together and said: Before I am delivered up to them, let us sing an hymn to the Father and go forth to that which lieth before us. He made us therefore make as it were a ring, holding one another's hands, and Himself standing in the midst He said: Answer "Amen" unto Me. He then began to sing an hymn and to say: Glory be to thee, O Father. And we, going about Him in a ring, answered Him: Amen.

'*Glory be to Thee, Word (Logos): Glory be to thee, Grace. Amen.*

Glory be to thee, Spirit: Glory be to thee, Holy One; Glory be to thy glory. Amen.

We praise thee, O Father; we give thanks to thee, O light wherein darkness dwelleth not. Amen.

97

A DANCE

'Now, whereas we give thanks, I say:

'I would be saved and I would save. Amen.
I would be loosed and I would loose. Amen.
I would be wounded and I would wound. Amen.
I would be born and I would bear. Amen.
I would eat and I would be eaten. Amen.
I would hear and I would be heard. Amen.
I would be thought, being wholly thought. Amen.
I would be washed and I would wash. Amen.
Grace danceth, I would pipe. Dance ye all. Amen.
I would mourn. Lament ye all. Amen.
The Ogdoad singeth praise with us. Amen.
The Twelve dance on high. Amen.
The Whole on high hath part in our dancing. Amen.
Whoso danceth not knoweth not what cometh to pass. Amen.
I would flee and I would stay. Amen.
I would adorn and I would be adorned. Amen.
I would be united and I would unite. Amen.
A house I have not and I have houses. Amen.
A place I have not and I have places. Amen.
A temple I have not and I have temples. Amen.
A lamp am I to thee that beholdest me. Amen.
A mirror am I to thee that beholdest me. Amen.
A door am I to thee that knockest at me. Amen.
A way am I to thee a wayfarer. Amen.

'Now answer thou unto my dancing. Behold thyself in me who speak, and, seeing what I do, keep silence about my mysteries.

'Thou that dancest, perceive what I do, for thine is this passion of the manhood which I am about to suffer. For thou couldst not at all have understood what thou sufferest if I had not been sent unto thee as the Word of the Father. Thou that sawest what I suffer sawest me as suffering, and, seeing it, thou didst not abide but wert wholly moved—moved to make wise. Thou hast me as a bed; rest upon me. Who I am thou shalt know when I depart. What I now am seen to be, that I am not. Thou shalt see when thou comest.

'If thou hadst known how to suffer, thou wouldst have been able not to suffer.

'What thou knowest not, I myself will teach thee. Thy God am I, not the God of the traitor. I would keep tune with holy souls. In me know thou the Word of Wisdom. Again with me say thou: "Glory be to Thee, Father; glory to Thee, Word; glory to Thee, Holy Ghost."[1] And if thou wouldst know concerning Me, know that with a word did I receive all things and I was no whit deceived. I have leaped; but do thou understand the whole and, having understood it, say: "Glory be to Thee, Father. Amen."

'Thus, my beloved, having danced with us, the Lord went forth.'[2]

The connection of this passage with the 'witch-dance', though it cannot be proved in the sense that a Euclidean theorem can be proved, is reasonably obvious. At the least it points to the existence, within about a century of Christ's death, of a ritual among a section of the Church itself which conformed to this formula. And though the *Acts of John* were rejected (by the second Council of Nicaea) at the end of the eighth century, it is probable—or, at least, possible—that this dance and these words persisted, either in the original or in a modified form, in the liturgy of the Manichaeans and the Cathars, into the Middle Ages and beyond.

Two further points in the hymn call for notice. The first is that no hint is given as to what *actions* are attributed to Jesus or what it was that called forth the command: 'Seeing what I do, keep silence about my mysteries.' That it was connected in some way with suffering is suggested both by His reference to it later in the narrative: 'That suffering also which I showed unto thee and the rest in the dance, I will that

---

[1] Cf. 1 John v, 7—an interpolation in the canonical epistle.

[2] *Acts of John* in M. R. James's translation of *Apocryphal New Testament* (1924).

it be called a mystery,' and by the implication that by suffering in a certain manner it is possible to neutralize pain. And it may be that this was one of 'the secrets of the witches' which they refused to divulge even under torture and fortified by which they went calmly to—and even voluntarily embraced— death by fire.

The second point is that the opening of the passage quoted —'the lawless Jews, who also had their law from the lawless Serpent'—and the reminder after the dance: 'Thy God am I, not the God of the Traitor,' by emphasizing the Gnostic dualism give a clue to the confusion of the terms 'God' and 'Devil' in 'witch' terminology. The conventional explanation that the God of the pagans became the Devil of the Christians is misleadingly simple. It was rather that, to orthodox Christian thought, the Jehovah of the Old Testament was the God and Father of our Lord Jesus Christ, whereas to Gnostic thought the Jehovah of the Old Testament was the Demiurge, Satan.[1] Gnostics, no less than Christians, worshipped the God and Father of our Lord Jesus Christ; they differed only in refusing to equate him with the Semitic Yahweh.

The Christian God, therefore, in so far as He was 'Jehovah' was, to the Gnostics, the 'Devil', whereas the Gnostics, in so far as they worshipped a God which was avowedly not the Christianized Jewish God were naturally accused by their opponents of a similar 'Devil' worship. But, in many trials for heresy and witchcraft, both sides were using 'God' to express the same Reality (and, to a large extent, the same practical if not theoretical theology). This in part explains the

[1] 'They ascribed to him the authorship of the whole, or the greater part, of the Old Testament. They found there, side by side with the eternal spiritual law, the code of an imperfect and transient morality; worse than all, they found there passion, revenge and cruelty ascribed to the Most High. It is not possible to read the remarkable letter of Ptolemy to Flora without perceiving that Old Testament exegesis was the real strength of Gnosticism. It was so powerful because it was so true. On this one point they retained their advantage to the last. The facts were in the main as they alleged, and the right explanations depended on principles equally foreign, at that time, to Gnostic and to orthodox.'—Bigg: *The Christian Platonists of Alexandria.*

difficulty in correctly interpreting the Christian accounts of trials—in particular that of Joan of Arc.

In general however the members of the Cult accepted the Christian appellation of 'Devil' for their God, as making for clarity. The priest—as God's representative—in each 'coven' was known as the 'Devil'; and at the head of the whole hierarchical structure was the supreme 'Devil' who like the Pharaohs of Egypt, was regarded as the incarnation of God and who, like the Slain King, was sacrificed for his people.

3. The Devil

Since 'devil' is a word so potently charged with associations it has become almost impossible to use it neutrally, its true meaning must continually be borne in mind as a corrective. The 'devil worshipper'—whether Gnostic, Manichaean, Cathar or 'witch'—in no sense said: 'Evil, be thou my good.' He worshipped the principle of Good in an exalted and even in a Puritan sense. (Indeed the 'Puritan' analogy is a convenient one for mentally combating false associations. The Cathars were 'the Pure'.) And in repudiating the God of the Christians, he was repudiating, in his own mind, only the Demiurge.

There may, indeed, have been those who actually worshipped the principle of Evil knowingly. Within the dualistic philosophy this was logically possible, since in an unfinished strife the final victory might be to Ahriman. But these were probably an infinitesimal minority, and the deliberate worship of evil had less foundation in fact than in the propaganda of the Church against the witches. Taken at its sharpest, the 'worship of Satan' (as the Christians described it) was by the witches themselves understood and intended as the worship of Lucifer, the principle of Light.

It is, once the confusion of terminology is understood, at least comprehensible that, in the eleventh century, worship of the 'Devil' could exist within the bounds of apparent orthodoxy in the Church itself; and indeed, with the theological system founded on the pseudo-Dionysius, it must have been difficult to say with certainty which conception of 'God' was in fact 'orthodox'. In particular, the Dionysian definition of a bishop had considerable analogies with the cult conception of a 'devil'.

The eleventh-century idea of a bishop differs not only in degree but almost in kind from that of the state-appointed organizer and financial administrator to which the name is applied in the twentieth century. For, as the Dionysian theologians taught and their hearers believed, the highest order in the ecclesiastical Hierarchy is directly linked with the lowest in the Heavenly. 'The most interesting link in the chain is that which joins the two parts—that is, the Bishop or, as Dionysius prefers to say, the hierarch. . . . In the hierarch the heavenly forces are concentrated; and in his overflowing "goodness" he permits these forces to flow through his administration of the sacraments and his symbolic actions, to all who are set under him. He is the "God-filled and divine man", possessor of the sacred Gnosis; it is through him that the different orders of the Ecclesiastical Hierarchy are purified and perfected. He holds the same position in the Ecclesiastical Hierarchy as God in the Heavenly. He is, so to speak, God on earth.'[1]

As the Church's conception of a Bishop was couched in terms which would be easily understood by a member of the Old Religion venerating his 'Devil', so there is also found in orthodoxy the same ascetical practices which distinguished heresy.

On the surface, all the logic of asceticism lay with the dualists. The Manichaean 'had one great advantage over the Christians, namely, that he provided a much more secure dogmatic basis for asceticism. The Christian ascetics, in condemning natural feelings and appetites, were constantly hampered by their theory of God as Creator of the universe in

[1] Nygren: op. cit.

general and man in particular; the distinction which they were obliged to draw between human nature as such and human nature in its present corrupt state gave rise to endless difficulties. On the other hand, the Manichaean dogma that humanity is of Satanic origin, however shocking it may be to modern sentiment, greatly simplifies the problem'.[1] And there are still to-day as there always have been, Christian thinkers who have contended that the whole ascetical side of Christianity is a perversion of the teaching of Him Who on earth had the reputation of being 'a gluttonous man and a winebibber' as well as incompatible with a true understanding of God the Creator and the implications of the Incarnation.[2] Rightly understood, of course, the Christian view of asceticism as voluntary reparation for sin has a totally different motive from the dualist's concern with personal salvation, but the practice of medievalism, with its ascription to the ascetic of superior sanctity merely because of his negations, was undoubtedly a weapon by which the Church sought to counter the heretics and was itself almost as much a deviation from orthodox dogma as the heresy itself. Not even the most fanatical apologist for Christian asceticism would deny that from the beginning the impact of pagan thought and practices has been considerable; and nowhere was the difference between them harder to discern than in the eleventh and twelfth centuries. When, after the murder of Becket, his hairshirt infested with lice and the marks of self-scourgings on his body revealed to the populace that he was a secret ascetic, the monks cried: 'See, see, he was indeed a monk and we knew it not' and 'none of them now doubted that he deserved to be called a martyr'. But a Cathar might legitimately have interpreted the facts in the opposite sense.

Thus both in Church and in anti-Church, actions and formulae could be interpreted in a variety of ways. Equivocation is everywhere. The practice of asceticism might mean

[1] A. A. Bevan in Hastings' *Encyclopaedia of Religion and Ethics.*
[2] For the whole subject see Hardman: *The Ideals of Asceticism* (1924).

that a man was a sincere and specialized type of Christian; or it might mean that he was a secret Cathar. A Bishop might be a 'Devil' and might—as in the case of Ranulf Flambard, Bishop of Durham during the reign of Rufus, the son of a witch and an avowed pagan—so consider himself. Becket's description of himself at the hour of his killing as 'sacerdos Dei' could mean either, if not in his own mind, at least in the minds of his hearers.

Certainty is rendered even more impossible by the very secrecy of the anti-Church. The essence of it was that it was esoteric; and a surface conformity with Christianity was not only prudent from the point of view of persecution; it was desired by the initiates on principle. This secrecy was maintained, whether by the witches meeting at night in forests or the Mithraists seeking initiation in caves on a desolate seashore in Wales or erudite Bishops interpreting the Catholic liturgy in a Cathar sense or the initiate in a company listening to the Grail romances or the Troubadour songs and understanding the point of them where their companions saw only an enthralling tale or a conceit of love.

Much of the literature seems to us, lacking the clue, something like the 'nonsense verse' that it has sometimes been called. But if we suppose that for centuries Christianity had been stamped out and persecuted, its sacred books destroyed and its liturgy forbidden, so that it lingered on only as a secret society, we can see how, for instance, the verse

> *Life-imparting heavenly Manna,*
> *Stricken Rock with streaming side*
> *Heaven and earth with loud hosanna*
> *Worship Thee, the Lamb Who died*

would appear a string of ludicrous paradoxes to all but the initiate, who would find in it a profession of faith, profound in its allusiveness. Something comparable is true of the secret anti-Church, which can never be thought of as a small cohesive body. Side by side with high philosophical ideas and

104

mystical speculations, there still existed the simple and un-learned to whom the 'Devil' was 'God' as the life-principle in its most primitive form. If the Sacred Dance of initiates led back to the Upper Room, the same dance among those of the 'outer circle' of believers led more obviously to the old rural *orgia*. Both were, indeed, comprehended in the same system of belief and practice, but there was little more affinity of *mind* between them than to-day, in the context of Catholicism, there is between an illiterate and superstitious Irish peasant woman telling her beads before a statue of the Queen of Heaven and a Jesuit theologian. The Old Religion was no less complex than the New.

4. *Rufus and Becket*

Our question may now be expressed in more precise terms. Were William Rufus and Thomas Becket the English (or Anglo-Norman) 'Devils' who were sacrificed in 1100 and 1170? Did they so regard themselves? And were they so regarded by the mass of the people?

My own belief is that Rufus undoubtedly was; that, as an avowed anti-Christian, he so regarded himself; and that he was certainly so regarded by the populace. The case of Becket is less simple, though there seems little doubt that he, like Rufus, was a 'Devil' in popular estimation. Several circumstances suggest that, though certainly not a pagan in Rufus's sense, he may have been a secret Cathar (a fact which, *at that date*, would not have been inconsistent with his canonization). And, in whatever sense he may have regarded his death, it would seem certain that it was a ritual killing of some sort, anticipated and acquiesced in by him. There may be some truth in the suggestion that he was acting as substitute for King Henry II.

The dates of the murders suggest a difference in atmosphere. The chief festivals of the witch-cult were pivoted on a May-November cycle—1st May, 1st August—the Gule of

August—1st November, and 2nd February. These celebrations indicated 'a division of time which follows neither the solstices nor the agricultural seasons' but which there is reason to believe was 'connected with the breeding seasons of the flocks and herds'. These festivals were Christianized as Roodmass, Lammas, Allhallows and Candlemas—but in the case at least of the May and the August festivals the Christian feast never became sufficiently important to drive out the pagan content.

The more important Christian cycle followed that introduced by Sun worship—Easter for the spring festival, St. John the Baptist for Midsummer, St. Michael for the autumn and Christmas for the birthday of the Sun in winter. But that the Christmastide festival was still deliberately paganized by a slight shifting of the date may be deduced from the evidence of the *Liber Poenitentialis*, which has already been quoted, that on 'the kalends of January' members of the cult were accustomed to go about 'as a stag or a bull'.

Rufus was killed 'on the morrow of Lammas' (2nd August); Becket 'on the fourth day before the kalends of January' (29th December). The former had a definite pagan significance; the latter was more equivocal.

The Divine Sacrifice took place on one of these festivals, apparently every seventh year. Whether the 'Devil' himself was always sacrificed or whether, as in the primitive pattern, he was in certain circumstances allowed a substitute, cannot in the nature of things be ascertained with any certainty. There is only the testimony of the members of the cult and the evidence of the Inquisitors that the sacrifice did take place, though in later centuries (the sixteenth and seventeenth, for example) a horned animal was usually killed in place of a human victim. During the medieval period, under the Cathar enthusiasm for suicide, there would probably be little difficulty in obtaining human substitutes. But in the earlier centuries—and especially in exceptional circumstances—the King himself had to die.

That the year 1100 was looked upon as an exceptional year there can be no doubt. Freeman, the Victorian historian of the reign of William Rufus, unsuspicious of such factors as we have been considering, is made aware of this by the mere objective reporting of the old chroniclers. 'At least within the range of the Red King's influence, that year seems to have been marked by that vague kind of feeling of a coming something. . . . Coming events do cast their shadows before them in a fashion which, whether philosophy can explain it or not, history must accept as a fact. And coming events did preeminently cast their shadows before them in the first half of the year 1100. In that age the feeling that weighed on men's minds naturally took the form of portent and prophecy, of strange sights seen and strange sounds listened to. There is not the slightest ground for thinking that all these tales were mere inventions after the fact. . . . Man's minds were charged with expectation; every sight, every sound became an omen.'[1]

It is certain that the King's mysterious death 'on the morrow of Lammas' in the depths of a forest was, within a few hours, known in Italy and in more than one place in England. It is certain that it was expected by the victim himself who, though he spent his last night restlessly because of the weakness of the flesh, made no effort to escape his end.

[1] Freeman: *The Reign of William Rufus* (1882).

Chapter VII

WILLIAM RUFUS

1. The Red King

William, surnamed 'the Red', was the third and favourite son of William the Conqueror, himself the bastard son of Duke Robert, 'the Devil' of Normandy. Rufus ascended the throne of England at the age of thirty on his father's death in 1087. During the thirteen years of his reign he showed himself a brilliant soldier and an efficient administrator. Witty and blasphemous, he was an avowed enemy of the Church and the unanimous disapproval he earned on this account from the ecclesiastical chroniclers has resulted in his being a singular example of a 'Bad' King, in the child's history-book sense. The legend of his accidental death while hunting in the New Forest—the result, so it is usually averred, of an arrow aimed by his favourite, Walter Tirel, at a stag—is one of the historical stories known to most readers from childhood, and takes its place in popular lore with the date of the battle of Hastings and the matrimonial adventures of Henry VIII. The very potency of the legend in part accounts for the fact that few characters in history are less known. That he was a 'bad' king, accidentally, though deservedly, shot on a hunting expedition is a most misleading epitome; though the statement that he was known as 'the Red King', that he was the grandson of the Norman 'Devil', that he was an open pagan and that he met his death mysteriously at Lammas-tide in a forest contains a series of, by now, recognizable clues.

The more one studies Rufus, the more impressive do the

clues become. 'From the beginning to the end', writes Freeman, 'there is a kind of glamour about the Red King and all that he does.' This judgement is the more remarkable because the great historian of the Normans is, on the whole, bitterly hostile to the King. He, no less than the child, classes him as 'Bad'. But such a simple reading will not, in the end, square with the facts.

He has to admit that Rufus was a portent of a new age. He was the incarnation of the spirit of 'chivalry'. 'To no man who ever lived was the whole train of thoughts and feelings suggested by those words (the spirit of chivalry) more abidingly present than they were to the Red King. It might be going too far to say that William Rufus was the first gentleman . . . but he was certainly the first man in any prominent place by whom the whole set of words, thoughts and feelings which belong to the titles of knight and gentleman were habitually and ostentatiously thrust forward. . . . When William plighted his word as *probus miles*, no man kept it more strictly. . . . Without fully taking this in, we shall not easily understand the twofold light in which Rufus looked to men of his own age, in whose eyes clearly he was not wholly hateful. . . . In William Rufus we have not only to study a very varied and remarkable phase of human nature; we have also to look on a man who marks the beginning of a new age and a new state of feelings.'[1]

All that this background of 'chivalry' implies we know—or at least are in a position to appreciate—far better than Freeman. Of itself, this objective testimony would link Rufus with the line of development we have been following; but there is other evidence to reinforce it.

2. His Name

Why 'the Red King'? The explanation usually given—that it was a nickname he owed to his ruddy countenance—is, on the face of it, scarcely satisfactory. If this were indeed the

[1] Freeman: op. cit.

reason, it must be a unique tribute to complexion—the more so since 'unlike most other names of the kind, his surname is not only used by contemporary writers, but it is used by them almost as a proper name'. And 'the second William is yet more emphatically the Red King than his father is either the Bastard or the Conqueror'.[1]

But red—the colour of blood—is and always has been all over the world pre-eminently the witch colour. At least from the days of the Pharaohs, when the salute to the Incarnate Sun was: 'Life! Blood! Health! Pharaoh! Pharaoh! Pharaoh!' it had been specifically associated with the Sun cult. More pertinently, 'with regard to the ancient Egyptians, we have it on the authority of Manetho that they used to burn red-haired men and scatter their ashes with winnowing fans, and it is highly significant that this barbarous sacrifice was offered by the kings at the grave of Osiris. We may conjecture that the victims represented Osiris himself who was annually slain, dismembered and buried in their persons that he might quicken the seed in the earth'.[2] The oxen which were sacrificed were also red—and so meticulously was this insisted on that a single white or black hair found on one immediately disqualified it for sacrifice.

There is no need to labour a point so well attested or a symbolism so obvious; and there can be no reasonable doubt that the mere phrase 'the Red King' would bear this inference to thousands of his subjects. It was even clearer than his grandfather's surname 'the Devil'.

One of the most surprising events of his reign was the immediate reception of him as King by the English, who were bitterly hostile to his father. As the 'Red King' of the Old Religion he would however have a natural claim on their allegiance. After his death, it was the common people who mourned him; and the contemporary chronicles insisted that as his dead body was taken from the New Forest to Win-

[1] Freeman: op. cit.
[2] Frazer: *Golden Bough*.

chester, followed by the peasantry, the blood dripped to the earth during the whole journey. This, which is still the folk-legend in those parts to-day (I have myself often walked on the path through a country field which is still called Kings-way), is an actual impossibility; but it is consistent with the belief that the blood of the Divine Victim must fall on the ground to fertilize it.

3. His Oath

Freeman notes, without understanding the implications of, Rufus's favourite oath—the oath which he never broke—and remarks that it is introduced into episodes in which it appears irrelevant. This oath was: 'Per vultum de Luca'—'by the Holy Face of Lucca.'

The full meaning of the 'Holy Face of Lucca' has yet to be unravelled by historians. This mysterious figure represents Christ reigning from the Cross, clothed in a 'colobium'—a garment with short sleeves, which is obviously the sacred robe of the Zoroastrians and which is admitted to be the earliest form of the 'dalmatic' which the Emperors Commodus and Heliogabalus wore as priests of Mithra on ceremonial occa-sions. The posture of the feet, which are not nailed, indicates the willingness of the Passion. The robe is embroidered with the figures of the Elect saints.

According to the conventional version of the legend, the face of Christ is that carved by Nicodemus and bound to the mast of a ship which, set afloat without rudder or crew, reached the shores of Tuscany and drifted up the river Ser-chio to Lucca.

The image dates from 783 and throughout the Middle Ages was regarded as a palladium by the Lucchese. This date, coinciding with the second great wave of Manichaeism in its Paulician form in the eighth century suggests that its signifi-cance is not to be found by regarding it merely as a pious Christian relic; and this is confirmed by the fact that 'Saint Voult-de-Lucques' was the name given to all crucifixes in

111

which the Figure was clothed in a similar fashion. It is possible indeed that the later form of crucifix—the naked, dead Christ —was introduced as a result of the Manichaean heresy, since the dualists could see in the Luccan crucifix the symbol of their doctrine that Christ, as man, was not crucified. The *Acts of John* contains a long conversation between Jesus and John at the time of the Crucifixion, while the 'body' of Jesus was still on the Cross. The esoteric interpretation of the Cross implicit in it is too intricate to be treated here, but some idea of it may be gained from the following extract: 'This cross of light is sometimes called the Logos by me (Jesus) for your sakes, sometimes Mind, sometimes Jesus, sometimes Christ, sometimes Door, sometimes a Way, sometimes Bread, sometimes Seed, sometimes Resurrection, sometimes Son, sometimes Father, sometimes Spirit, sometimes Life, sometimes Truth, sometimes Faith, sometimes Grace. And by these names it is called as towards men; but that which it is in truth, as conceived of in itself and as spoken of unto you, it is the marking off of all things, and the firm uplifting of things fixed out of things unstable, and the harmony of wisdom and indeed Wisdom in harmony.'[1]

The 'Holy Face' might thus legitimately be regarded as symbolic of something other than the Passion understood in the orthodox Christian sense. And Lucca itself was a centre in which syncretism had been carried to extreme lengths. Its most ancient church, dedicated to St. John, was built on the site of the pagan temple and the columns of that temple had been utilized in the building of it. The tomb of St. Frediano, patron saint of Lucca in early times, was a pagan sarcophagus containing bas-reliefs of the doctrines of the Mysteries. His altar was reputed to have been miraculously drawn to the city by two 'wild cows'—which, in effigy, are undoubtedly Mithraic Bulls.[2] The elaborate font in which the figure of Christ the Ram-bearer is prominent, seems, from the de-

[1] James: *Apocryphal New Testament.*

[2] See sketch in M. Stokes: *Six Months in the Apennines* (1892).

112

scriptions of it, to have an esoteric significance—the 'serpent', for example, is represented as a dragon, and the cupola is sculptured to represent the seasons.

Nor is the ascription of the crucifix to Nicodemus without a certain relevance. The conventional story that Nicodemus carved the Face from a portrait miraculously imprinted on a handkerchief preserved by (or given to) St. Luke at the time of the Passion is an obvious variant of the better-known story of St. Veronica. Its purpose would seem to be to bring St. Luke in connection with Lucca—and some of the older writers mistook Rufus's 'per vultum de Luca' for an oath by St. Luke's face. But the bringing together of Nicodemus and 'Luke' can be explained in a simpler fashion. One of the most important books in the Gnostic version of the Bible was 'The Gospel of Nicodemus', the second part of which is concerned with Christ's descent into the Underworld. The author is that Luke—Leucius—who is also the author of the *Acts of John*.

Taking all these things together, it does not seem unreasonable to suppose that 'the Holy Face of Lucca' was patient of more than one interpretation and that Rufus's invariable oath, though apparently sworn on a crucifix, was in reality taken in quite another sense.

4. *His Associates*

There are at least three names in the story of Rufus's reign which, though of no outstanding importance in the politico-historical approach, are of some moment in the aspect we are considering. One is the son of Cadivor, Prince of Dyfed (the Pembrokeshire peninsula of Wales), who, in the Red King's wars against the Welsh, remained friendly to the King; one was William IX of Aquitaine, who came to the aid of Rufus in his campaigns in France and who eventually pledged his Duchy to the English King: and one was Helias of Maine, with whom Rufus was both perpetually at war and on terms of personal friendship.

His relations with Helias, at least, constitute a mystery from the conventional historians' point of view—his release of Helias, when he had him in his power, with the words: 'I give you leave to do all you can, and, by the face of Lucca, if you ever conquer me I will not ask for any grace in return for my favour to-day'; his sudden abandonment of the war with Helias; and the white robe which, on one occasion, Helias put on to enable him to go freely into an enemy castle (a garment which gave him the nickname of 'the White Bachelor').

There is one episode in particular, during one of the occasions when Rufus was besieging Helias, which Freeman finds inexplicable and 'wholly unexpected'. 'He gave orders for a general attack on the castle on the next day (Saturday). The Sabbath morning dawns; the warriors are vying with one another in girding on their weapons and making ready for the attack. Then a pious scruple touched the hearts of some of the elders of the host. Certain unrecorded wise men crave of the King that out of reverence for the Lord's burial and resurrection, he will spare the besieged both that day and the next and will grant them a truce until Monday. In other words they demand the observance of the Truce of God. The King gives glory to God and gives orders that it shall be as they wish; nothing shall be done against the castle on either Saturday or Sunday; on Monday the attack shall be made.'[1]

As the matter is recorded, the incident is indeed inexplicable in the light of Rufus's known paganism. But if the wise men are 'Wise Men' in the technical 'witch' sense and the Sabbath was Lammas—the event occurred in August—and Helias, as both his name and his 'white robe' suggest, was a fellow-member of the cult, it becomes immediately comprehensible. Could this be established with certainty, it would be overwhelming evidence in favour of the general thesis. It is a conjectural possibility only, but it supplies an explanation of facts which are otherwise admittedly inexplicable.

With William IX of Aquitaine, we are on more certain

[1] Freeman: op cit.

ground. This young man, who was Rufus's friend, ally and companion-in-arms for the last two years of his life, was also William VII, Count of Poitou. It is as 'the Count of Poitou' he is best known, at least in literary history. He was the first of the Troubadours, a man, according to the chroniclers, brave and accomplished, but irreverent and immoral. His poetry is the first Troubadour poetry which is known and among it is an example of the 'enigmatic' verse which enshrined the Catharist doctrine. In this 'Song of Nothing', however, the belief in over-ruling Destiny is sufficiently explicit to make its trend plain enough for those who care to interpret it.

If Rufus's friendship with the Count of Poitou shows him in close contact with the Troubadours, his connection with the son of Cadivor in Wales brings him in touch with the Grail, for this Bledri was, as has been previously noted, the author of the first Grail romance which communicated to initiates the Mithraic mysteries.

To these three names may be added a fourth, that of Rufus's chief Minister, whom he made Bishop of Durham and his personal 'chaplain'—the Ranulf Flambard who was the son of a priest and a witch and whose 'fiery' surname had implications of the same order as Rufus's own.

5. His Character

That Rufus was not a Christian—at least in the orthodox sense—is apparent from all his actions and his persistent attitude to the Church, to which he maintains the character of persecutor. He jeered openly at Christianity; delighted to set Jews and Christians to discuss the merits of their respective creeds; consistently plundered Church lands; openly declared that neither St. Peter nor any of the saints had any influence with God and that he would ask none of them for help; and was angry if anyone added the usual reservation 'if it be God's will' to anything that he ordered to be undertaken.

He regarded himself in a way which can only be construed as 'divine', of which the later developments of that 'divinity' which 'doth hedge a king' are but shadows. He compared himself with Alexander the Great—and the comparison was generally admitted, with the additional speculation as to whether or not he was also the reincarnation of Caesar.

Rufus was unmarried and his name was never connected with that of any woman. The open homosexuality of his court, with its crowd of 'effeminati' and their new fashions of long hair, extravagant manners and luxurious dress was hardly less reprehensible than the King's blasphemies in the eyes of the ecclesiastical chroniclers who deplored particularly the courtiers' habit of shaving 'so that their beards should not chafe their friends when they kissed'.

Of the King's personal behaviour nothing certain is known, though Tirel is spoken of as his 'familiar' and it is impossible that he should be excluded from the general assumption. But this, however it may have affected the judgement of his Christian opponents and of posterity, does not seem to have weighed heavily with his contemporaries among whom he was 'the peer of the most renowned of those Nine Worthies the tale of whom was made up only in his own day'.[1] And when, after his death, his brother Henry, with his crowd of mistresses and bastards, started a 'moral reform' of the Court his success—and, indeed, his attempt—was both partial and temporary.

It would seem, then, considering all these indications, not unreasonable to connect William Rufus with the cult—or heresy—we have been discussing. He was the first great representative of 'chivalry'; he was notoriously celibate; he was consistently an opponent of orthodox Christianity, compared by John of Salisbury to Julian the Apostate. 'As regards the character of Rufus, which Freeman acknowledges he cannot estimate, it displays all the Pagan virtues. Rufus was a dutiful son, an able and competent ruler, a faithful friend,

[1] Freeman: op. cit,

116

a generous enemy, recklessly courageous, lavishly open-handed, and was never known to break his plighted word.'[1]

6. *His Death*

It remains only to consider certain factors in the story of his death—a death which, from whatever point of view it is considered, must remain largely a mystery.

The traditional version—that one of his attendants, drawing a bow at a stag had missed the animal, with the result that the arrow killed the King—has one point of interest. It was the way in which Rufus's nephew, Richard, had actually met his death in the New Forest earlier in the year. It was an accidental misfortune, the repetition of which might be regarded as bordering on the eccentric. But the manner of that death, which was public, would at least establish the credibility of the method if announced of Rufus's death, which was secret. It was a circumstantial explanation for the un-initiate, which would not be seriously questioned, especially as young Richard's death had raised an outcry and his slayer had escaped vengeance only by becoming a monk.

In the account of Rufus's death, there are other details which to any initiate would suggest something less than an accident. The death is consummated in the depths of a forest at sunset on the site of an ancient church—and thus, presumably, a pre-Christian holy place; the King's slayer stands under an elder tree; the King partakes of a kind of last sacrament of herbs and flowers; in the majority of accounts he is slain by an arrow loosed by his intimate, Tirel, after Tirel's hesitation and the King's command: 'Shoot, in the Devil's name, or it will be the worse for you', and the arrow was one of two special ones, designed not for the cross-bow but for the more deadly arbalest, which he had given to Tirel that morning with the remark: 'It is right that the sharpest arrows should be given to him who knows how to give death-bearing strokes (lethiferos ictus) with them.'

[1] Murray: *God of the Witches*.

117

That the King himself and not a substitute should be sacrificed may not have been unconnected with the date—1100—and the feeling of apocalyptic doom which hung (though less heavily than in 1000) over the realm. This superstitious dread must have been overwhelmingly accentuated by the great tide which, on the day of the new moon at the beginning of November 1099 (that is to say, on the November 'Sabbath') came up the Thames, obliterated houses and villages and swept away men, oxen and sheep. The great Dragon of the Sea was loosed, hungry for prey.

The expectation of Rufus's death at Lammas is attested by many stories; and it is certain that the King himself was prepared for it.[1] Perhaps the most curious is that version of the 'King's dream' in which Rufus went alone into a chapel in a forest, whose walls were hung with purple tapestries of Greek workmanship, embroidered with ancient legends. Suddenly all these disappeared and the walls and altar stood bare. On the altar the King saw a naked man, whose body he tried to eat. But the man said 'Henceforth thou shalt eat of me no more' and vanished. In another version it is, even more significantly, the body of a stag (for the stag was a cult horned-animal of almost equal importance to a bull) which changed to that of a man. The stories of the dream—whether Rufus actually had it or not—leave no doubt as to the contemporary view of the nature of his death.

On the night of the death, in Belgium, Hugh, Abbot of Cluny, was told that the King's life was at an end. On the day of the death (that is to say, before it had actually happened) Peter de Melvis in Devonshire met a countryman bearing a dart, who said to him: 'With this dart your King was killed to-day.' Anselm in Italy received the news in less time than travel was possible from a 'young and splendid' man who told the clerk on guard at Anselm's door that the strife between the Archbishop and the King was over.

The conflicting accounts of Rufus's burial in the sanctuary

[1] See for details Appendix SS in Freeman, op. cit.

of Winchester Cathedral—where the plain black stone facing the altar still forms symbolically the most dramatic tomb in England—can be reconciled satisfactorily only on one hypothesis. The ecclesiastical writers insist that no bell was rung, no mass was said, no offerings were made for his soul. The poets—the early Troubadours—insist equally that the body, strewn with flowers, was buried with such worship, such saying of masses as no man had heard before or would hear again till the day of doom. Both series of accounts admit the enormous concourse of people present, and it would appear that the rites which the Christian authorities intelligibly refused to the pagan king were carried out by priests secretly of his own faith (which would present no difficulty) to the satisfaction of the mass of the people who knew well enough the importance of the death of the 'Devil'.

Chapter VIII

THOMAS BECKET

1. The Angevins

The death of Rufus—if the foregoing interpretation be allowed—is comparatively simple in so far as it is an issue between the Old Religion and the New. But the death of Becket in his cathedral of Canterbury seventy years later 'on the long night of the winter solstice' contains elements which suggest the Cathar rather than the pagan. One is conscious of a complete change of atmosphere. It is impossible to 'christianize' Rufus; but there is nothing incongruous in Thomas Becket becoming 'St. Thomas of Canterbury'.

The essential connecting link, however, is still the pagan sacrifice of the Slain King, the theory that Becket no less than Rufus was an English 'Devil'. That it was the Archbishop and not the King who died presupposes the validity of the thesis that, from Saxon times onwards, the relationship between King and Archbishop had been of such a nature that either might fulfil the role of 'Devil',[1] and that, though Rufus failed to make Anselm, Henry II succeeded in making Becket his substitute in the sacrificial murder. Becket was given boundless privileges in return, but when the time came in 1163 (the ninth seven-year cycle after Rufus) he refused to die and fled

[1] The historical examination of this thesis would require another essay in itself; but it will, I hope, be clear that, by the very nature of the powers of an Archbishop, there can be no theoretical objection to it. For further information on the point readers are referred to the works of Miss Margaret Murray.

for his life. Seven years later, he returned to England, having become reconciled to Henry, just in time for the death which he, like Rufus, anticipated. Round this simple framework is a mass of subtle detail which is more Cathar than pagan.

And in the seventy years between the deaths, Catharism, with its Troubadours, had spread over Christendom like a flame. In particular it was associated with the Angevin house which now ruled England. Henry of Anjou, who ascended the English throne as Henry II in 1154, at the age of twenty-one, was born in the castle of Le Mans, the capital of Helias, the 'White Bachelor', who was his great-grandfather and had died only twelve years before his birth. Henry II's wife, whom he married at the age of nineteen, was Eleanor of Aquitaine, grand-daughter of the Troubadour 'Count of Poitou' and herself famous as a patron of the Troubadours.

When Henry came to England to be crowned, leaving Eleanor in Normandy, he brought with him Bernart of Ventadorn, the 'greatest of the Troubadours' who, while in England, wrote to her (his 'Magnet' as he describes her) one of his most perfect lyrics.[1]

Of the sons of Henry II and Eleanor, Henry 'the Young King'—who was brought up by Becket—was also a patron of the Troubadours and the lament on his death by Bertrand de Born is probably the best known of all Troubadour poems.[1] Their third son, Richard—our Richard Coeur-de-Lion—was himself a Troubadour and our childhood story of Richard and his fellow-Troubadour Blondel conveys more truly the sense of the period than the more sober details of the taxation of England to pay for the Crusade which adults are apt to consider more specifically 'History'.

Nor was the Angevin house alone in its devotion to Catharism. In that age—the eve of its greatest flowering—no less than thirteen of the reigning princes of Europe were of 'the

[1] Translated (in prose) by B. Smythe in *Trobador Poets* (1929).

[2] Also translated in *Trobador Poets*, but the best-known rendering is Ezra Pound's 'Planh for the Young English King' (in *Selected Poems*, 1928).

Brethren' and there can be little doubt that, in this at least, princes and people were at one. It would be a mistake to see only a picturesque pageant of knights and poets and allow the exuberance of 'romantic' figures to detract attention from the quiet faith of the people who were actuated by the same beliefs and who, to the uninstructed eye, might pass for model Christians. St. Bernard, their persecuting opponent, has left on record this picture of them: 'If you interrogate them, nothing can be more Christian; as to their conversation, nothing can be less reprehensible and what they speak they prove by deeds. As for the morals of the heretic, he cheats no one; he oppresses no one; he strikes no one; his cheeks are pale with fasting; he eats not the bread of idleness; his hands labour for his livelihood.'[1]

In the circumstances, it would be more surprising, if Henry and Becket were not initiates of the cult than if they were; and if the adherence to (and almost worship of) Becket by the common people was due less to their approval of his ecclesiastical policy than to their belief that he was their 'Devil'.

2. *Thomas of London*

Thomas Becket—Thomas of London as he was more generally known by his contemporaries—was born in 1118. His education began at the age of ten at Merton Priory and ended after a study of theology in Paris at the age of twenty-two. After a short career as a notary, he took service with Theobald, Archbishop of Canterbury, and for twelve years was employed by him in a diplomatic capacity. In 1154—the year of Henry II's accession—he was rewarded for his abilities by being made Archdeacon of Canterbury and, to qualify himself for the post, took deacon's orders. The following year, Henry appointed him Chancellor—an office in which he made the interests of the Church so subservient to the King's lay policy that he was accused of 'plunging his sword into the

[1] Quoted in H. C. Lea; op. cit., vol. I,

bowels of his Mother'. His interests were notably secular and it was as diplomat and soldier that he distinguished himself. He directed campaigns, led a company of knights and, on one occasion, engaged in single combat and unhorsed a French champion.

For the seven years between 1155 and 1162, an inseparable friendship bound Henry II and his Chancellor. At the beginning of it 'Thomas was a man of 38 with a wide experience of the world and a considerable knowledge of man; Henry was only 22, with the brilliance, the audacity and the instability of youth. . . . It is the custom to speak of their friendship as the mutual attraction of two like spirits. This is a little wide of the truth. Henry was drawn to a man who was old enough to be his counsellor and young enough to be his companion. Thomas responded just as ardently to a king who rewarded him with affection and gave him a wide field for the exercise of his great abilities. . . . From the beginning they worked together as a single man and a single mind. There was no constraint in their companionship. . . . They were in and out of each other's houses at all times. They had no shame at fooling about together in public, so that their intimacy was known to all.'[1] At least in the early days of that intimacy, it was Becket, not Henry, who was the dominant partner.

In the year 1161, Henry entrusted his heir, the six-year-old 'Young King' Henry, to Becket to be brought up in his household. The same year, Theobald, Archbishop of Canterbury, died, after asking in vain to see the King and the Chancellor, who remained in France. In 1162, Henry sent the Young King, under Becket's charge, into England to receive homage from the nobles to ensure his succession—an act which was to be reinforced by the boy's coronation. As the See of Canterbury was vacant, Henry decided to make Becket Archbishop in order to perform the ceremony. In spite of Becket's protests, remonstrances and warnings that it would be the end of all friendship between them, Henry persisted in this

[1] Speaight: *Thomas Becket* (1938).

plan. On the eve of Trinity Sunday, 1162, he was ordained priest; next day he was consecrated Bishop, and in the presence of the Young King enthroned Archbishop of Canterbury.

His first major function as Archbishop was to attend in state the Council which the Pope had called at Tours at Easter 1163 to discuss the Cathar heresy. Though this Council was 'against the Manichaeans or Albigenses', it was not until the great Lateran Council of 1215 that a specific exposition of the faith of the Church against the Cathars was made and the doctrinal position defined. Becket's orthodoxy appeared impeccable, but he was concerned mainly on other matters. He obtained a renewal of privileges for Canterbury Cathedral; presented a life of Anselm by John of Salisbury and made a petition for Anselm's canonization.

On his return to England, he had his first quarrel with the King over a matter of Royal encroachments on ecclesiastical privileges, and from this moment (at the Council of Woodstock in the July of 1163) till the end of his life, he and Henry remained, with the exception of one brief period of reconciliation in 1170, as bitter enemies as they had hitherto been inseparable friends.

The details of their controversy, centring on the limits of Royal jurisdiction over 'clerks' in minor orders, is a matter of political history. In this, the 'Constitution of Clarendon', Becket's defiance of the King on behalf of 'his Order' at Northampton in 1164 and his flight from England to sanctuary in France are of some importance and are treated fully in any history book. There, too, can be read the simple explanation that, on his consecration, Becket became a changed man, reversing his life's policy, and henceforward defied the State on behalf of the Church as enthusiastically as he had previously plundered the Church on behalf of the State.

Though it would be obviously rash to assert that this was not the true reason and that the logic of events is not in fact as simple as it seems, it is at least possible to hold that it is not the full explanation and that the psychology of it (especially when it is remembered that Becket did all in his power to decline the Archbishopric and warned Henry in advance of the consequences) is somewhat too simple.

In the quarrel over the privileges and rights of the Church, the majority of the Bishops—and the best of them—were on the King's side, not on the Archbishop's. And Becket was made Archbishop for the specific purpose of crowning the Young King—a matter of supreme symbolic and mystical importance. The King of England could be crowned only by the Archbishop of Canterbury; the 'Young King' must be crowned by Thomas Becket. This was the King's point and, however one may interpret what lay behind it, it cannot be disputed that the argument was sufficiently powerful to cause Becket to give way in spite of his inclinations and his better judgement. So much may be admitted without necessarily endorsing the theory that the 'Young King's' intended coronation by Becket at the end of 1162 was to be followed by Becket's death in 1163—a sequence of events which would have ensured the boy of the unquestioned loyalty of the mass of the people, since it would have implied that he was the new 'Devil', appointed and consecrated by the old before his sacrificial immolation.

The coronation of the Young King remains, even from the most objective historical point of view, a determining factor in Becket's murder in 1170. As Becket had not crowned him in 1162, he remained uncrowned for the next eight years. But by the fateful year 1170, Henry would delay no longer. The young man, now sixteen, was crowned in London by the Archbishop of York, in spite of the energetic protests of Roger of Worcester, a kinsman of the King, and 'against the desire and opinion of nearly all in the kingdom'. Becket's first act, when he was reconciled to Henry and returned to England to die, was to excommunicate and suspend the Bishops who were concerned in it; it was the news of this excommunication which threw Henry into a fury, fed by the

Archbishop of York's comment: 'My lord, while Thomas lives, you will not have peace'; it was to force him to rescind his sentence that the knights who killed Becket ostensibly set out and, a few moments before his death, they importuned him to give absolution to the bishops—which, to the end, he refused.

3. Henry and Becket in 1170

The reconciliation of Henry and Becket took place in the summer of 1170. The King saw Thomas when he was far off and ran to meet him, bareheaded. He drew him apart and they spoke together as though their quarrel had never been. During the four months before the Archbishop left for England, they were on terms of friendship once more and their political differences appeared to be settled. But one thing— the one thing which Becket desired—Henry would not give— the Pax, the ceremonial 'Kiss of Peace' exchanged after the Consecration at Mass. Henry was willing to give the formal, secular kiss, which would have the force of a promise in the political arrangements they had agreed on, but he would not give the Pax.

At their last meeting—at Amboise in the autumn—Becket tried to trap him into it by attending Mass with him. Henry thereupon ordered the Mass of the day to be changed to a Mass for the Dead (where the Pax is never given). But after the Last Gospel had been read, Thomas kissed the Book and handed it to the King with the words: 'My Lord, now that I have come to you in your own land, give me the Kiss for the sake of the time, the place and in consideration of your oath.' But the King turned away in confusion and told him that he should have the Kiss another time.

This curious episode, puzzling if not inexplicable on any conventional hypothesis, is suggestive enough in the light of Catharism.

In the first place, it is relevant that the 'Last Gospel'—the Prologue of St. John—was read at all; for it was at this date

Church of Love!

a local and sporadic usage and, even then, was usually said by the celebrant on his way back from the altar to the sacristy. The Prologue was, as we have seen, not unconnected with the heresy; and if the Church later ordered the reading of it as an orthodox counterblast to the Gnostic interpretation, the practice in the early days was more likely to denote Cathar than Catholic leanings.

In the second place, a kiss given after the Last Gospel would not, technically, be the Pax at all. The ceremony in which the reading of the Prologue of St. John was followed by a ritual kiss was the sacrament of the Cathars where, as we have seen, it was bestowed on the initiate, who, thereafter, had a forty days' fast—an *endura*—in the course of which many 'brethren' committed voluntary suicide.

Is it not at least possible that what Becket wanted was not to receive the sacramental Kiss, but to *give* it to Henry? If they were both—or had been in earlier days—Cathar initiates, it is likely that Henry as the younger man owed obedience to Becket. The receiving of the Kiss implied obedience and, had Henry accepted it, at that point and with those implications, it might well have been he, not Becket, who would have been dead before forty days were over.

As it was, Becket bowed to his fate. 'My lord,' he said as he took leave of Henry, 'we shall never meet again on earth.' He also told the Archbishop of Paris that he was going into England to die. For this prognostication, there was no shadow of apparent reason, however historians, wise after the event, have tried to find one in the political situation. What it signified was surely Becket's acquiescence in his role. And Henry's understanding of it may equally have prompted his action of holding Becket's stirrup for him as he mounted—a humility flagrantly out of keeping with Henry's character but 'if Becket had consented to be the Divine Victim, the real king would then, according to custom, be subordinate for the time being'.[1]

[1] Murray: *God of the Witches.*

127

4. *The Murder in the Cathedral*

Of the manner of Rufus's death nothing is known; for Becket's death there are five eye-witness accounts and numerous contemporary versions of varying credibility. But the truth is still not easy to arrive at. All the main accounts are printed, compared and annotated in the first volume of Abbott's *St. Thomas of Canterbury* and no one who has not studied them can have any idea of the lack of historical foundation for most conventional reconstructions of the famous episode.

The tendency 'to honest, zealous and affectionate "lying" may be illustrated from a letter written immediately after the murder by the Archbishop of Sens to the Pope. . . . The writer speaks of him (Becket) as "standing before the altar", "embracing with his hands the cross that he had been wont to bear before him", offering himself up "between the horns of the altar and the cross" and lastly as "praying for his persecutors, adding also and most passionately supplicating that at least his household might be preserved unhurt". . . . This letter is a tissue of small inaccuracies, all dictated by the best of motives, affection for the dead and a desire to honour his name, but still very misleading'.[1]

The confusion is increased by the enormous number of representations of the scene in art, in which, contemporary though they are, every detail is wrong; by pious attempts to parallel his martyrdom with the passion of Christ and the consequent invention of words and actions to sustain it; and by later historians' addiction to what has been aptly termed 'the fallacy of the Fitness of Things'. The difficulty is not lessened by the fact that the scene is so traditionally famous that it is one of the few episodes in English history which is 'known' by nearly everyone—an honour it shares with Rufus's death.

If, for example, I should write: The Archbishop, caring

[1] Abbott, op. cit.

128

nothing whether he was murdered or not, refused the advice of the monks to remain safely in his palace, but insisted on proceeding into the Cathedral. Clad in his sacerdotal garments, he moved majestically in solemn procession, his primatial cross borne before him, until he reached the High Altar. He was standing before it when his murderers entered, calling 'Where is the Archbishop?' His companions, at the approach of danger, fled, but Becket replied calmly: 'I stand here at the altar for you to see; what is your will?' For answer they advanced upon him, their axes in their hands, but one with a drawn sword. Becket faced them like a soldier and commanded them to leave the House of God which they were sacrilegiously outraging. Thereupon one of the knights struck at him—a blow which Becket warded off with his arm, from which the blood began to flow. This was the signal for the end. The knights closed in on him and the Archbishop fell, his body bleeding from many wounds. With his last breath he commended himself to his Saviour Jesus Christ and begged forgiveness for his murderers—if I should write this, everybody would recognize the scene and hardly anybody would realize that not only is every statement in it false but that the total effect is the exact opposite of the truth.

As far as one can reconstruct the proceedings by weighing and comparing all the evidence, the events of the afternoon seem to be as follows. After Becket had again predicted his approaching death, the four knights who were to kill him called at his palace, where he received them courteously. They charged him with the intention to flee; he retorted in some anger and his last words to them were the promise: 'You will find me here.'

When they left him, however, the monks forcibly carried him into the cathedral 'in spite of his resisting and struggling and refusing' and his fear that, if he took refuge in the church, the knights would refrain from killing him. He wore no sacerdotal garment, but his canon's cloak and he did not order his cross to be borne. Once in the church, he commanded the monks to unbar the door so that the knights could enter unimpeded at the appointed time—sunset. He refused to go to the High Altar, but turned aside into the north transept and stood by a pillar. When the knights called to him, he replied: 'I am here, the Priest of God' (sacerdos Dei) and ascended four steps to await them. He spoke to the first knight, Reginald, in the intimate second-person singular saying, 'You are my man (i.e. vassal)'. Reginald replied by striking off the Archbishop's cap with his hand. He then raised his sword and Becket bent his neck forward and commended himself to 'the doom of God, to St. Mary and to blessed Dionysius'. Each knight struck one blow and all the blows were directed at the same place—the crown of the head where the holy oil had been poured in his anointing as Archbishop. At the third stroke, the victim fell 'taking pains that he might fall in honourable fashion, covering himself down to his ankles with his pallium' and being careful to fall towards the north. He was killed by the fourth—and last—blow which almost severed his crown, having made no resistance to death

Through the confusion in the Cathedral, with an attempt at defence by one of the monks, and with retainers and citizens frightened and clamouring spectators in the winter darkness, a kind of ritual emerges plainly enough. Its exact nature is, of course, impossible to tell. But that it was apparent to contemporaries may be deduced from the efforts made to falsify the details of it.

5. The Omissions of John of Salisbury

One of the most curious discrepancies is that, of the fifteen authorities, all except two either omit the date, 1170, or give it incorrectly as 1171. 'The full explanation of these errors', says Abbott, 'must be left to chronological experts.' The chronological explanation, of course, is that at least two systems of reckoning dates were in use—one beginning the year at the feast of the Annunciation (25th March), the other at

Christmas (25th December). It is noteworthy that 'Gervase, the twelfth-century monk of Canterbury, bewailed the confusion arising from various computations; he himself had wavered between the systems of Christmas and the Annunciation before finally adopting the former for his *Chronicle* and even then he made a concession to the more popular system for one famous event, the death of Thomas Becket on 29th December 1170.'[1] Certainly to contemporaries the 1170 would immediately indicate the possible nature of the killing.

Another circumstance of the same kind is that one of the eyewitnesses took pains to record that Becket ascended *four* steps and that a later writer specifically mentioned that it was *seven*—which makes Abbott ask in surprise: 'Are we to suppose that Fitzstephen was so keen an observer that he noted the exact number of steps to be "four" and thought it worth recording, simply as a statistical fact, and that Herbert, who was not present, knew of Fitzstephen's tradition and thought it worth contradicting?' If 'symbolical' is read for 'statistical' the answer (in the light of the significance of the number four) is surely in the affirmative. 'Seven' could be, and had been, 'Christianized'. 'Four' could not.

One of the men, who was with Becket in the cathedral at the time of the murder, is careful to omit both the date and the number of steps. This was John of Salisbury, one of Becket's closest friends and counsellors, who was in a position not only to know exactly what passed but also to understand the meaning of it.

It was John of Salisbury who, earlier in the year, had written to Becket reproaching him for his consultation of augurers and witches; and he had, for some years at least, had no illusions as to the nature of Becket's beliefs. In 1159 he had dedicated to him his 'Polycraticus' or 'Courtier's Trifles and Philosophers' Footprints', a patchwork of quotations whose source he professes to believe that Thomas will recognize without being told. In the section on magic arts and astrology,

[1] C. R. Cheney: *Handbook of Dates* (1945),

he opposes the doctrine of Necessity by the conventional Christian arguments but 'he expresses doubt whether Thomas will be convinced by his arguments or whether he will not laugh up his sleeve at so clumsy an attempt to refute so formidable a doctrine'.[1] He instances, also, occasions on which Becket has consulted both an aruspex and a cheiromancer and warns him that such men are not to be trusted.

In the light of this knowledge, it is not as surprising as Abbott seems to think to find that John of Salisbury's account of the murder is 'most meagre'. This description, indeed, is a notable understatement. His account is a masterpiece of omissions and falsifications. It is to him that we owe the deliberate lie—which found its way into books and pictures —that Becket died 'in front of (coram) the altar'. He is careful to insist that Becket fell 'with body straight', whereas the other accounts make it clear that he was careful to fall to the right—that is to say towards the North, or as Garnier's poem put it 'in the aisle of the North and facing the North did Thomas suffer death'.

His omissions are not less pointed than his falsifications. In addition to his silence about the date and the steps, he has nothing to say about the interview of the knights with Becket, of Becket's reluctance to go into the Cathedral and the reason for it, of the approach of the knights, and of the actual murder, which he avoids by remarking that 'pity does not permit the enumeration of the details one by one' of the slaying.

That he does not give the names of the murderers may be, certainly, as Abbott says, because 'he was a man of temperate disposition, favouring moderate courses, and he may have thought that no good could be done by heaping execrations on them'. But the other falsifications cannot be so explained; nor, since he was intimate with Becket and an eyewitness of the murder, can they be dismissed as later historical embroi-

---

[1] Quoted in Lynn Thorndike, op. cit., from *Epistola* 297 (Migne: cols. 345–6).

deries. They are, surely, calculated efforts to blur a pattern which was understood well enough at the time, even if it is not understood at all to-day.

6. *Echoes of the Cult*

Some of the indications that the murder was, in some sense, the cult rite we have already noticed—the recurrence of the number four, the day and the time, the precision of the action. These are independent of the hints of Becket's own belief. There are two more which, comparatively insignificant in themselves, yet reinforce the general conclusion. One is the words attributed to one of the knights : 'He wished to be king ; he wished to be more than king ; just let him be king.' The other is his choice of his place of death—on the North.

It is probable that those with knowledge of Masonic secrets are in a position to estimate, even if they could not divulge, the full meaning of this. Some of the symbolism of architecture is common knowledge, but it is in this department of esoteric knowledge that the uninitiated feels more baffled than in any other. But at least it can be seen and said that in all dualist philosophy, and explicitly in Manichaeism North and South have distinct and opposed significations. According to Mani, one of the expressions of two forces of Good and Evil was the Two Trees—the Tree of Life and the Tree of Death. The Tree of Life stands in the North ; the Tree of Death in the South. The superiority of the North—if not its essential difference—survives in the Christian ritual which assigns the 'Gospel-side' of the altar to the North, in contradistinction to the inferior 'Epistle-side' on the South.

Becket took his stand, deliberately, by the great central pillar in the north transept which, at festivals, was hung with curtains and draperies. This was the place where, according to a member of his household, 'he had long ago beheld himself crucified in a dream'. Whatever his motive for 'turning aside to the northern part of the church', and choosing a pillar rather than an altar for the place of his death, his action led him to die where, ritually, the Divine Victim might have been expected to die—a circumstance which has presumably actuated the writer of the *Saga* years after his death and canonization to assert: 'He turneth to the East, towards that altar of Our Lady whereat he had stood.'

The *Saga* also, with equal falsity, asserts that Becket's headgear, which was struck off by Reginald, was a mitre. The metamorphosis of the 'cap' into a mitre was often copied in later art (it is already a mitre in the illumination in the Carrow Psalter painted about fifty years after the murder) and again the change reinforces the mystery of the nature of the 'cap' worn on this occasion. There had been no satisfactory explanation of it; and it may be relevant that, in the earliest illumination (about 1190) it is represented in a form which is recognizably that of the famous Phrygian Cap of Mithra.[1]

When Becket was dead, Hugh of Horsea, a subdeacon, went up to the corpse, and, thrusting his sword into the head, scattered the brains on the pavement. Almost immediately the efficacy of the spilt blood was recognized as a cure by the people, who at once paid Becket what can only be considered divine honours. Miracles were said to have begun even before the body was buried. When the body was examined, there was found, in addition to the marks of his secret asceticism, which have already been mentioned, a letter 'about his imminent death', which he had foretold openly enough and which was known in many places—Devonshire, Argentan, Jerusalem— a few hours after it occurred.

The attitude of the people to the Archbishop leaves little doubt of the light in which they considered him. Like Rufus, he was almost worshipped by them, yet he seems more remote from them than the Red King. On his return to England on 2nd December—a date subsequently kept as the feast of the Regressio Sancti Thomae—the poor in multitudes swarmed

[1] See illustrations in Tancred Borenius: *St. Thomas Becket in Art* (1932).

to meet him at Sandwich and made his six miles' ride to Canterbury a triumphal progress without parallel. It is difficult to believe that they were passionately interested either in the question of the precedence of the See of Canterbury over York in the matter of the Young King's coronation or in that of the right to try criminous clerks (in which their own interests were represented rather by the King's policy than the Archbishop's).

Abbott's comment that 'Thomas himself did not put forth the poor but "his Order" as the good cause for which he was ready to die; but still the poor felt that their cause was bound up with his' is obviously conditioned by the nineteenth-century liberal-humanitarian view of the Middle Ages; yet it contains more truth than the Victorian writer realized. The common people did indeed know that their 'Devil' had come to die for them.

In what light Becket regarded himself must remain a mystery; but his conduct at his death makes it hardly credible that he was not aware, at least, of the part he was playing. In terms of his theology, the blood sacrifice was open to more than one explanation; and there can be no doubt that he died for his God. If the fact that, in 1172, a possible Cathar could be canonized may appear incongruous to the faithful, a parallel case may allay alarm. It would be impossible to-day for anyone denying the dogma of the Immaculate Conception of Our Lady to be considered orthodox, far less to be canonized. Yet, as we have seen, both St. Bernard and St. Thomas Aquinas explicitly repudiated this doctrine, which was not made *de fide* till 1854, and their right to sainthood is not thereby impugned. In these matters, the date is the determining factor; and Becket, canonized in 1172, was at liberty to disbelieve many things (including transubstantiation) which were not defined till the Lateran Council of 1215.

At the beginning of this essay was quoted the reminder that 'the great Gnostic thinkers were heretics, not in the sense that they left the high-road, but in the sense that the track along which they went was not the direction along which the high-road was afterwards constructed'. At the end of the quest, this distinction must be reiterated, for it applies particularly to the death of St. Thomas of Canterbury.

That death draws together the threads we have been following. It remains a mystery, even in the popular sense. And the matters underlying it—Love and Sacrifice—are the profoundest mysteries of all.

III
THE THEOLOGICAL
IMPLICATIONS

Chapter IX

THE HERESY

---

1. The Puritanism of 'The Pure'

The exact nature of Catharist beliefs is impossible to determine with any certainty. On the one hand, the heresy seems to include sects differing in details; on the other, the main stream is fed from many sources; but the over-riding difficulty is to be found in the circumstance that, as the near-contemporary records of the Church and the Inquisition are the testimony of enemies—though, by making due allowance for animus and ignorance, they yield some of the truth—the jealously guarded secret of the cult is a secret still.

The matter is further complicated by the partisanship of certain later writers who have concentrated exclusively on one aspect only of the movement; and it is enlightening to examine their emphasis before endeavouring to outline more fully the probable theological position of Catharism.

In 1838, the then-famous Anglican controversialist, George Stanley Faber, Prebendary of Salisbury, published *An Inquiry into the History and Theology of the Ancient Vallenses and Albigenses, as exhibiting, agreeably to the Promises, the perpetuity of the sincere Church of Christ*. His starting-point is Bossuet's famous argument that the doctrine of the Catholic Church subsists in four points, the connection of which is inviolable. The first point is that the Church is visible; the second that It always exists; the third that the truth of the Gospel is in It always professed by the whole Society;

the fourth that It is not permitted to depart from Its doctrine. But to Bossuet's contention that these are the distinguishing marks of the Roman Catholic Church, Faber opposes the thesis that not only are they lacking in that body but that they are actually present in the Albigensian heresy. He admits Bossuet's claim for the necessity of a 'visible Church', but finds that phenomenon in the Middle Ages not in the Roman allegiance but in the Cathar movement which he sees as the medium by which 'the Reformed Churches of the sixteenth century stand connected with the Primitive Church'.

The Cathars would certainly have agreed with him, since they taught that there are two churches, the one merciful— the Albigensian Church of Christ which retains that faith without which no one can be saved; the other the merciless Church of Rome, which is the Mother of Fornication, the Temple of the Devil, the Synagogue of Satan, within which everyone is irretrievably damned.

Bossuet also had anticipated this line of attack and blocked it in advance by remarking that 'the Albigenses and their predecessors the old Paulicians were Manichaeans, who through a long succession of ages handed down the impious heresy of a paganizing Orientalism and who, therefore, cannot without great want of prudence be claimed by the Reformed Churches of the sixteenth century as a branch of their theological predecessors'.[1]

The conventional Protestant method of extrication from this dilemma, as used by Faber's predecessors, was to contend that 'in the south of France two entirely different classes of religionists, the one composed of what sound Protestants would deem pious orthodox believers, the other consisting of the relics of emigrated Oriental Manichaeans were, in the twelfth and thirteenth centuries, from the town of Albi, alike denominated Albigensians'. Faber's honesty and research alike prevented him from adopting this defence and he quite

[1] Faber; op. cit. quoting Bossuet: *Hist. des Variat.*, XI., 7–10.

rightly insists that such a division did not in fact exist. To controvert Bossuet, he was therefore forced to deny the Manichaeism and in his book is at pains to demonstrate that 'the perpetually self-contradicting charges of Manicheism brought against (the Cathars) by writers of the Church of Rome are entirely unsubstantiated and thence unworthy of the least credit'.

Even if Faber's readers were convinced by his arguments, scholars of a later age have found them untenable. The Manichaeism of the Cathars is too obvious to be overlooked and fifty years after the publication of Faber's book, H. C. Lea in his great *History of the Inquisition in the Middle Ages* was able to take it for granted—'the Manicheism of the Cathari or Albigenses was not a mere speculative dogma of the schools, but a faith which aroused fanaticism so enthusiastic that its devotees shrank from no sacrifice in its propagation'.

There remained scholars who, if prevented by the facts from following Faber's line of attack were not disposed to admit the simplicity of Bossuet's orthodox defence. The Rev. H. J. Warner in *The Albigensian Heresy* (1922) writes: 'The resemblance between the Dualism of Gnosticism and Catharism is obvious. Each taught both a modified and an absolute Dualism; but a closer study shows us that whereas with Gnosticism (and particularly Manicheism) this dogma was fundamental, with Catharism it became more and more subordinate to discipline and conduct.' At which one can only ask how, if they taught an 'absolute dualism' this cardinal dogma could possibly avoid being 'fundamental', however 'subordinate to conduct' it might appear in its effects. Nor does the author's attempt at differentiation on a wider basis— 'Gnosticism was esoteric, Catharism exoteric; Gnosticism was intellectual, Catharism spiritual'—convince one of anything but his instinctive sympathies for Faber's thesis.

The importance of this approach is that it serves to throw into vivid relief one aspect of Catharism which in modern times tends to be ignored—that the 'Pure' were Puritans who could be and have been proudly claimed as forerunners, not tacitly disowned as heretics, by Protestant Christians. For Catharism indubitably was, among other things, a moral protest against a corrupt hierarchy. The depths of that corruption are a common matter of history, however greatly, at times, the exaggerations of Protestant propaganda may have brought their credibility into question among the unscholarly. It is sufficient here to quote from a source unlikely to be biased against Rome—Pope Innocent III's letter to the Archbishop of Narbonne and its clergy: 'Blind, dumb dogs that cannot bark! Simoniacs who sell justice, absolve the rich and condemn the poor! They do not even keep the laws of the Church. They accumulate benefices and entrust the priesthood and ecclesiastical dignities to unworthy priests and illiterate children. Hence the insolence of heretics. . . .'

He might also have added: 'Hence the strength of heretics!' and, in the eyes of some, then and later, their justification.

The anti-Catholic will naturally tend to make the most of this circumstance and see in the movement nothing but—in Lea's phrase—'the natural outcome of anti-sacerdotalism seeking to renew the simplicity of the Apostolic Church'. The pagan elements he will prefer to regard as the inimical slanders of its traducers. In reaction from this one-sided interpretation it is possible to swing too far to the other extreme and, in stressing the pagan content (as I have deliberately done in the first part of this essay) to overlook the fact that there was in Catharism—as we have seen that St. Bernard himself bears witness[1]—a high morality, a nobility of life and a code of ethical behaviour which put contemporary Catholics to shame. It is not all the story, or even the most important part of the story. It may also be said—since no one has ever claimed that Christians had a monopoly of morals—that it is not really relevant. But as to ignore it would be to falsify the perspective, the reminder of Faber's forgotten claim for the Cathars is not without value.

[1] See *supra*, p. 122.

THE HERESY

2. The Cathar Trinity

But what were the Cathar theological beliefs, as far as they can be reconstructed? Their general dualistic doctrine has been sufficiently noticed, but, since they habitually used Christian terminology, it may be instructive to approach their theology by way of their interpretation of the Trinity.

We have it on the authority of Reinéri Saccho, who was once a Cathar but later became an Inquisitor, that they held that the world and all that is in it were created by the Evil God, whose servants were the Old Testament Patriarchs, whose sacraments and Church were the existing Catholic sacraments and Church and whose inspired writings were the Pentateuch and the historical books of the Old Testament.

The Good God, they held, had created only a limited number of good spirits, but even many of those had been turned from their allegiance to him by the Evil God by means of a beautiful woman. When the spirits thus fell, the Evil God provided them with tunics (their bodies) in order to make them forget their first estate. Death was merely the passing of the spirit of one tunic to another (here is the Pythagorean doctrine of transmigration) until it came into a tunic in which it would be saved—that is to say, the body of a Cathar. It would then return in that tunic to Heaven.

This dualism ensured that there could be no Trinity in the Christian sense, for the Good God could never unite with flesh. The impossibility of the interpermeation of good and evil which the Incarnation (on their view of the flesh) involved was reinforced by their belief in the inequality of the Persons. The Father, they held, was greater than the Son and both than the Holy Spirit.

Nevertheless from other sources[1] it appears that as regards the Second Person of the Trinity the Cathars did not hold

[1] I have followed here Warner's analysis and sources in his first volume of *The Albigensian Heresy*. Though I have disagreed above with one of his conclusions, I should make it clear that this scholarly book is the indispensable authority in English.

143

the strict Docetic views of Christ which characterized Gnosticism generally. They were prepared to admit *an* Incarnation, but contended that Christ was created sinless in Heaven, and in His already perfect nature of body, soul and spirit was born *in* the Virgin Mary.[1] That is to say, they substituted '*in* virgine' for '*ex* virgine' and adhered to the sequence given in the Johannine Prologue—'the Word was made flesh and (then) dwelt among us'—and not that of the Creed—'came down from Heaven and was made Man'.

There may, of course, have been some among them who interpreted that other sentence of the Prologue—'the Light shineth in darkness and the darkness overcame it not'—in the proper Gnostic sense that Christ, as Light, could not enter matter, which was Darkness, and that His human body was thus an appearance only; but there can be little doubt that their official doctrine admitted the reality of Christ's Humanity and Passion.

Their attitude to the Cross confirms this view. Whereas the early Gnostics, as we have seen, honoured the Cross as an esoteric symbol, the Cathars regarded it as a mark of shame and held that 'all holy crosses should be broken up and burnt, since that instrument by which Christ was so fearfully tortured and so cruelly put to death was not worthy of adoration, veneration or any other worship, but in revenge for His torments and death should be dishonoured with every kind of infamy, struck with swords and burnt'.[2] No man, they said, adores the gallows on which his father was hanged.

[1] But even here a difficulty of interpretation exists, for it also appears that they taught that the Virgin Mary was not and is not a real woman, but is 'True Penitence' whereby people were born into the Cathar Church. The Virgin Mary was also understood as the Cathar Church itself and the 'Ave Maria' was said with that connotation. The relationship of Our Lady, thus esoterically understood, with the Lady of Troubadour poetry is obvious and, as we have seen, not without its relevance to Becket's dying commendation of himself to 'The Doom of God, St. Mary and Blessed Dionysius'.

[2] This was the teaching of Peter de Bruis, who was active between 1100 and 1130. Though strictly a tenet of the 'Petrobusians' only, it seems to be distinctive of Catharism in general and may also have its

Since the Incarnation was not held in the Christian sense, it followed that there was a difference of essence (*substantia*) between the Three Persons—a distinction which the Cathars based on two other Johannine texts. They contended that Christ's words: 'If ye loved me, ye would rejoice because I said I go unto my Father, for my Father is greater than I' meant that the Father was greater than the Son; and that His promise: 'It is expedient for you that I go away, for if I go not away the Comforter will not come unto you, but if I depart I will send him unto you' meant that the Son was greater than the Holy Spirit and that the Holy Spirit was not operative in the world until after the Ascension.

The doctrine of the Holy Spirit is probably essential to the understanding of Catharism; and it is exactly here that the investigator is most conscious of inability to penetrate to the heart of the teaching. The authority for as much as we know is Moneta of Cremona, a Dominican of the thirteenth century, whose work against the Albigenses is the only contemporary systematic investigation of the heresy. Moneta claims that his information came from Cathar writings (subsequently, of course, destroyed), but it is doubtful whether, even if he contrived to act as an unbiased reporter, the full interpretation of the doctrines was ever committed to writing by the Cathars.

According to Moneta, the perfect man was made in the image of God in the tripartite nature of body (*corpus*), soul (*anima*) and spirit (*spiritus*). Because of sin, his *spiritus* returned to Heaven, leaving every man on earth imperfect because consisting only of *corpus* and *anima*. Nevertheless the *spiritus* of each man is the guide and guardian (rector) of his *anima* and is restored to him by the Paraclete (*the* Holy Spirit) by the laying-on of hands. That is to say, the gift of the Holy Spirit which an initiate received by the imposition of hands

---

place in the death of Becket—the insistence of the latest chronicler on the bearing of the primatial cross before the Archbishop, a circumstance not mentioned by the earlier authorities.

was not, as with the Christians, the Holy Spirit Himself, but the man's own *spiritus*.

It is here that there seems a hiatus in the evidence, for the gift of the *spiritus* must have meant more than, thus baldly stated, it appears to mean. One needs an exact definition of terms and relationships, even interpreting it as the restoration to man of the Divine image by the return of the *spiritus*. It is not clear, either, whether 'the Holy Spirit' was consistently used by the Cathars as meaning the *spiritus* but by the Christians as meaning the Third Person of the Trinity, so that the heretics and the Inquisitors were using the same word in totally different senses, much as, in the witch trials, there was a confusion of the terms 'devil' and 'God'. One can sympathize with the exasperated complaints of the Inquisitors about the Cathars' evasiveness which made them, in conversation with Catholics, seem eminently orthodox. But, whatever their real doctrine was, it is clear that an inferior theory of the nature of the Holy Spirit in no way implied a dishonouring practice. To arrive at this conclusion, one has only to compare a Christian confirmation service, where the Holy Spirit is bestowed as it were wholesale in a conventional if not casual rite to children under twelve, with the Consolamentum (as the imposition of hands was called) of the Cathars.

3. The Consolamentum

This ceremony, as has been noticed earlier, was the only genuine sacrament of the Cathars and formed the initiatory rite of a 'Perfect'. For this reason alone none could partake of it but those who had already given evidence of long and loyal service to the sect. The vast majority—the 'Believers'—never received it at all; and even a large proportion of those who did postponed the reception until they were in what they supposed was their last illness.

The candidate prepared himself, if he were in health, by a rigorous fast. Before the ceremony, he was reminded by the officiating minister of the ascetic life he must henceforth lead, of the certainty of persecution and of the probability of torture and death. He was also warned that a lapse meant eternal damnation. The initiate then made the promises. These included abstention from meat, eggs, cheese, oil and fish[1] (and as he was never thereafter allowed to eat alone, there was some guarantee that the diet would be adhered to); never to touch a woman or to sleep unclothed; never to indulge any lust (though, apparently, he might satisfy the lust of the *flesh*, if sufficiently importunate, as long as he remained pure in *heart*); never to kill, never to lie or swear; and never to reveal the secrets of his faith.[2] Thereupon he made three obeisances to the minister (as the instrument of the Holy Spirit), after which he kissed the 'Text'—a book containing probably the Johannine Prologue. Then all present placed their hands on his head and shoulders, saying: 'We worship thee, Father, Son and Holy Spirit'; the minister prayed that the Holy Spirit, the Consoler, might descend on him; the Lord's Prayer was said, the Johannine Prologue read and the Kiss of Peace given. The initiate, now a 'Perfect', was then presented with that small cord to be worn round the body which, as we have seen, was descended from the Zoroastrian *kosti* and which was considered the hall-mark of a heretic.

4. The Four 'Sacraments'

If it were subsequently discovered that the officiating minister was in mortal sin (as a Cathar would define mortal sin), the Consolamentum was invalid. In making this incalculable

---

[1] Except, apparently, sacramentally. See infra.

[2] The frequent incompatibility between these latter promises may be illustrated by the circumstance that when required they often took a legal oath, since a refusal to do so would have revealed their belief and thus exposed them to the danger of death. Their justification was that, as they were filled with the Holy Ghost and doing his work, to injure or to end that work would therefore be the sin against the Holy Ghost which has no forgiveness. By the same argument they could guard the secret of their faith by perjury.

and disturbing provision, the Cathars were merely applying to their own sacrament the principle which had led them to repudiate the Catholic Sacraments—all of which they stigmatized as 'vain and useless' because administered by men whose morals were seldom better and usually worse than those of the recipient. That is to say, they denied the first principle of sacramentalism, without which no visible church could exist for an hour—the principle of which the most familiar definition is the title of one of the Articles of the Church of England: 'Of the unworthiness of Ministers, which hinders not the effect of the Sacrament.'

According to Saccho, they held that a good layman could and a bad priest could not absolve. According to Peter de Vaux-Sarnai, they derided baptism by water and the initiatory rite into the grade of 'Believer' included the following questions and answers: 'Do you renounce the cross which the priest made on you in your baptism on breast and shoulders and head with oil and chrism?' 'I do renounce it.' 'Do you believe that water works salvation for you?' 'I do not believe it.' The 'baptism' which the neophyte then received seems to have consisted in the minister breathing seven times in his face saying: 'Receive the Holy Spirit from Good Men' (though here again 'Holy Spirit' must have had its own particular meaning, differing from that in the Consolamentum).

Their Holy Communion was a commemorative meal only in which—according to the records of the Inquisition in Languedoc—its nature was specifically defined in the opening prayer over the bread, wine and fish: 'O Lord Jesus Christ, who didst bless the five loaves and two fishes in the wilderness, and blessing water turned it into wine: bless in the name of the Father, Son and Holy Spirit this bread, fish and wine, not as a sacrifice or offering, but in simple commemoration of the most Holy Supper of Jesus Christ and his disciples.'

Their attitude to Penance is not altogether clear, though, as has been mentioned, they denied absolutely the validity of the Catholic absolutions and asserted that sin after the Consolamentum was unforgivable. But they had a form of Penance in which the minister pointed out to the sinner how he had offended against Holy Scripture and added: 'I, being entrusted with the authority of the blessed apostles Peter and Paul, bid thee on behalf of our Lord Jesus Christ (Who instituted the holy sacrament of Penance in His Church)[1] perform such penance as I impose upon thee.' He added not 'I absolve thee' but 'May God forgive thy sins'.

Such Orders—Majors, Presbyters and Deacons corresponding roughly to Bishops, Priests and Deacons—as the Cathars possessed were executive and administrative merely, not sacramental; but ordinarily only a Major could administer Penance, preside at the Easter celebration of Holy Communion or bestow the Consolamentum. All grades were taken from the 'Perfect' and their appointment, apparently, depended on election by the local Cathar congregation, which was autonomous. But the succession of the Apostles was not confined to those in Orders, but extended to all the 'Perfect'. 'It was proved not by ecclesiastical pedigree, but by personal experience and responsive conduct. For it was the direct gift of the Holy Spirit to the individual and was not mediated through man. These Spirit-filled persons composed the True Church. It is less true to say that the heretics were "cut off from the Church" than that they deliberately repudiated and left the Church because it had forfeited its status by quenching the Holy Spirit, as was shown by its corruptions and persecutions. The loss of the Holy Spirit involved the loss of its power to excommunicate. Only those were successors of the Apostles who copied their life.'[2]

There is thus a sense in which the Cathars retained four of the Sacraments which their acceptance of the New Testament

[1] This is the formula given in the records of the Inquisition, but the portion I have placed in brackets is so at odds with the rest of the teaching that it is impossible not to suspect that it is either an interpolation or a deliberate attempt to mislead.

[2] Warner, op. cit.

made it impossible for them to discard. The evidence of the Apostolic practice of Baptism, Holy Communion, Penance and Orders was too patent to be ignored. At the same time they carefully emptied these practices of all genuine sacramental content and regarded them (as has probably been noticed by the reader) in a way almost identical with that of modern Protestants[1]. Had this aspect of their teaching been the essence of Catharism, the suggestion that it forms the link between the Reformed Churches and the nineteenth century conception of Apostolic times would be incontrovertible. But its distinctive quality is elsewhere. The clue lies not in their repudiations but in their assertions; not in their moral protest and—as they saw it—its logical justification, but in their own 'sacrament' and its consequences; not in their pre-Protestantism but in their neo-Gnosticism.[2]

5. The Endura

The Consolamentum, as we have seen, was, because of the terrible consequences of a relapse, postponed by the ordinary Cathar until he was mortally ill. When he was in this state, every inducement was offered to him after receiving the Consolamentum to end his life by any means other than direct

---

[1] The mixture of ancient and modern heresy has been pungently summed up by C. H. C. Pirie-Gordon in his *Innocent the Great* (1909): 'This singular gallimaufry contains several items on which (even among Christians of the present day) there is not an universal consensus of opinion, e.g., the Real Presence, Sacerdotal Authority, Extreme Unction, Holy Order, the Incarnation, the Resurrection, the Sign of the Cross and the Precise Epithets which are applicable to the Church of Rome. Others again will easily be perceived to be the merest echoes of heresies which were already obsolete in the thirteenth century, e.g. of flagrant Manicheism in the clause relating to the duality of the Deity, of Montanism in the singularly immoral regulations relating to matrimony. Others again, such as the doctrines of Baptism, on Oaths and Vegetarianism are a curious anticipation of more modern shatterpated infatuations. But what can we say of such incoherent and phantastic nonsense as the articles dealing with the Blessed Virgin... or legalizing lingering suicide?' This is an excellent example of the 'rational' approach to the problem.

[2] If indeed the two can be validly separated either then or now.

violence. This Endura, as it was called, took several forms. In one of them, the 'consoled' was asked whether he would be a martyr or a confessor. If he chose the former, a cushion was held over his mouth for some time and, whether he lived or died, he was held to be a martyr. If he preferred confessorship, he was deprived of food and drink for a certain period and, again, whatever the outcome he was considered a confessor.

Other forms of embracing death were by opening a vein in a bath or of drinking the juice of wild cucumbers mixed with powdered glass.

At this point there is hardly need again to stress that this fanaticism for death, which could best be appeased by judicial execution or ritual murder, immediately connects the heresy with the 'murder' of the Mithraic initiation and with the contemporary sacrifices of the witch-cult. Nor do we need the evidence of the belief of a Cathar community at Montfort as early as 1028 that 'death by illness or senile decay only showed that Satan was still master of the situation and could send the soul into another body'[1] to detect the age-old Gnosticism that inspired it. And we are hardly surprised to find that the terms in which the Christian apologists denounce Mithraism—that it was the work of the great counterfeiter, the Devil, himself (for human agency or plagiarism is never suggested)—are echoed nearly a millennium later by St. Bernard who, speaking of the Cathars, asks: 'By what name or title do you think you can call these? By none, for their heresy is not of man and they did not receive it through men. It is by the deceit of devils.'

---

[1] Warner, op. cit.

Chapter X

THE REPLY OF ORTHODOXY

1. Doctrinal Definition

In so far as the essence of Catharism was its Gnostic dualism, the Church's general theological answer was the same as it had been in the early centuries of the same struggle. The reader who wishes to study it in detail can find it in any handbook on the Faith, or, perhaps more speedily, in his own Book of Common Prayer where the epitome of it, the *Quicunque Vult*, the so-called 'Athanasian Creed', stands as his intellectual talisman against heresy.[1]

The Church's particular contemporary answer to the Cathars was given at the great Lateran Council of 1215, in which Catholic doctrine was crystallized by the seventy canons of Pope Innocent III.

The opening clause contains the doctrine of the Trinity and adds that all things, even the demons, were originally created by God—a direct and explicit denial of dualism.

There follows an exposition of the Catholic faith in the Incarnation, the Resurrection and Ascension of Christ's Body and Spirit, and in His Second Coming as Judge when

---

[1] It is interesting to notice that Protestant movements in the Church of England usually endeavour to minimize the importance of or even to discard the 'Athanasian Creed'. This is the less surprising when it is remembered that 'of the ancient creeds of Christendom, the *Quicunque Vult* is the only one which explicitly and unequivocally states the full Christian doctrine of God . . . We may question its suitability for recitation in public worship, but there can be no doubt of its value as controlling the *otherwise ambiguous* creeds of Nicaea and Constantinople'. (Hodgson: *The Doctrine of the Trinity* (1943): italics mine.)

152

all men will rise in their bodies—a specific refutation of the Gnostic view of matter as regards both Christ's Flesh and men's.

Then, insisting that there is only one Universal Church outside which none can be saved, the Council proceeded to that pronouncement for which it is generally remembered in history—the doctrine of transubstantiation. In the Church, Christ is both Priest and Victim. His Body and Blood are truly in the sacrament of the altar under the species of bread and wine. These are transubstantiated by Divine power, so that we may partake of His Body as He partook of our body. The sacrament can be consecrated by a priest only, according to the power of the keys.

Since the majority of the subsequent controversies of Christendom issue from this article (mainly because the laity usually misunderstand the technicalities of theological language—particularly 'substance') it obviously cannot be discussed here in a general sense. But the particular sense in which it was framed against the Cathars contains most of the clues. On the one hand, by precluding any view of the Eucharist as a simple commemoration and emphasizing that the mere utterance of the formula of consecration by a 'good man' is not sufficient for validity, it negatives every idea behind the 'Protestant' Cathar interpretation. On the other, by defining It in terms of bodily sacrifice, by insisting that Priest and Victim are identical and by relating the sacrificial act to mutual intercourse between Divinity and humanity, it took account of the 'pagan' content of Catharism and called in Revelation to correct and to explain the hypothesis of an instinctive naturalism. In this latter respect it should be remembered that the very extravagances of popular Eucharistic worship which characterized medievalism and which, in retrospect, so scandalize the scientific rationalism of modernity are best understood as an acknowledgment of the actual situation and beliefs with which the article was framed to deal. The corporal aspect of the Holy Sacrifice of the Mass and the worship of the Divine Victim were likely to be less incomprehensible to the friends of a Cathar consenting to the Endura or the followers of a 'Devil' about to die than to a twentieth-century Anglican discussing the merits of the 1662 Prayer Book rite.

On the subjects of other sacraments, the Council asserted that Baptism must be in the name of the Trinity but that, provided the invocation were correct, it was valid no matter who administered it; that those who received it obtained salvation but that, if they subsequently fell into sin, they could recover their innocence by true penitence. This destroyed the exclusiveness of the Cathars, condemned the theory that adult baptism was the only way of obtaining pardon, denied that there was any moment in life (e.g. after the Consolamentum or at the point of death) when forgiveness was impossible, and asserted the true sacramental nature of Penance.

On this matter a further canon—the twenty-first—introduced a new development specifically designed to check the spread of Catharism. For the first time in Christian history, auricular confession to a priest was made compulsory. Here again, as in the matter of Transubstantiation, the relevance of this now-conventional practice, which in modern times gives rise to certain criticism[1] can be properly assessed only by seeing it in its contemporary context. And there is little doubt that it was Innocent's most brilliant act of statesmanship. 'This was the greatest weapon devised against heresy.'[2]

Marriage and celibacy were dealt with in the canons which ruled that not only did virgins who lived a life of continence deserve salvation, but also married persons if they pleased God by a pure faith and good works. The celibacy of the clergy was reaffirmed and a more rigid observance of the rules

[1] Many non-Anglicans would agree, for example, that the Anglo-Catholic insistence that confession is voluntary is to be preferred to the Roman Catholic ruling that it is obligatory, in that the presence of an optional penitent is *ipso facto* evidence of the right disposition of his will.

[2] F. J. Foakes-Jackson: *Introduction to the History of Christianity* (1921).

enjoined; though, on the other hand, the canons of this subject were 'less violent in their tone than those of former synods' and 'the rule was admitted to be merely a local ordinance peculiar to the Latin church'.[1]

This careful insistence that clerical celibacy was a matter of discipline, not of faith (as, of course, it remains) is generally held to have been due to the desire of the Council to end the schism with the Eastern Church, where married priests were permitted. That this was one factor, and an important one, cannot be denied; but at the same time it is legitimate to see even here the influence of Catharism. By explicitly stating that clerical celibacy was not a matter of faith, it implicitly condemned the cardinal point of the heresy. Here, above all, the slightest deviation was dangerous, for it cannot have been absent from the minds of both parties that when the decisive contest with the married clergy had been fought out in Milan a century and a half earlier the allies of the great Hildebrand, the champion of celibacy, 'were themselves heretics who seem to have held Manichaean views resembling those of the Albigenses'.[2]

2. Practical Reactions

The definition of doctrine in 1215 can thus be properly regarded not as a general affirmation of the accepted faith so much as a particular answer to the Albigenses, as individual and contingent as was the sixteenth-century Council of Trent in relation to the Protestant Reformation. But the interaction of heresy and orthodoxy went far beyond official theological definitions. For what changed the face of Christendom was the practical means by which the Church turned the Cathars' weapons against themselves. The answer to the Troubadours and the 'Perfect' was the Friars. Adopting the ascetics' austerity of life, training themselves in dialectic as subtle and

[1] H. C. Lea: *History of Sacerdotal Celibacy* (Revised Edition 1907).
[2] Foakes-Jackson: op. cit.

speech as convincing, the Order of Preachers—the 'Dogs of God'—went out to controvert them by precept, argument and example; and the followers of the Little Poor Man of Assisi, with poetry and poverty, captured the imagination of the age. 'When the Church attacked the heretics by means other than fire and sword, she failed until the Dominicans copied their methods and the Franciscans their morals.'[1] Thus the description of St. Francis as 'the Troubadour of God' is more exact than many who use it symbolically may realize; and the whole story of the mendicant orders, in both their rise and their decay, is almost unintelligible apart from some knowledge of Catharism.[2]

The influence of the heresy is also traceable in certain practices adopted by the Church at this time. Two—the spread of a somewhat extravagant Eucharistic devotion and the inauguration of compulsory confession—we have already noticed as the outcome of the Lateran Council's decisions. Two others—the growing cult of the person of Our Lady (that 'mariolatry' which Protestants deplore) and the reading of the Johannine Prologue at the end of every Mass, so that its Christian content was plain and was, presumably, visibly emphasized by the priest's genuflection in honour of the Incarnation at the words 'And the Word was made Flesh'— were the answers to the Cathar interpretation of 'St. Mary' and the Gospel of the Consolamentum.

How far these were effective answers, it is impossible to determine. The very similarity of the practices may have defeated their own end; for the policy of annexing anti- or unChristian rites and beliefs is doubled-edged, and, as in the days of Constantine both Christians and Mithraists could conscientiously acknowledge the Invincible Sun, so in the

[1] Warner, op. cit.

[2] 'In their decay', because in the end they seem to have absorbed many of the errors which in the beginning they were formed to combat. The development of this lies outside the scope of this essay, but the connection between Catharism and the excommunicated Fraticelli rewards examination.

Middle Ages an analogous technique may have allowed an extreme ambiguity within the Church.

3. The Joachists

The danger of such an analysis as I have tried to make is that this pervading sense of ambiguity may be lost and the issues appear as far more clear-cut than in practice they were. The balance may perhaps be righted a little by a reference to the teaching of Joachim of Floris who, born about 1132 and dying in 1202, was roughly a contemporary of Becket.

Though after his death, the Lateran Council of 1215 condemned certain of his writings on the Trinity as heretical, it refrained from condemning him and actually approved the order of Floris which he had founded; and five years later the Pope promulgated a Bull formally recognizing Joachim as orthodox and forbidding anyone to injure his disciples.

The basis of Joachim's mystical teaching was 'the Eternal Gospel', founded on the passage in the Revelation of St. John which speaks of the angel 'in the midst of Heaven, having the everlasting gospel to preach unto them that dwell on the earth, and to every nation and kindred and tongue and people'.

There were, according to Joachim, three states of the world, corresponding to the Three Persons of the Trinity. The first was the age of the Father, the age of the Jewish Law and of Fear. The faithful in this age—the age of St. Peter—were the Servants of God.

This first dispensation was brought to an end by the coming of Christ which inaugurated, to the accompaniment of bitter persecution, the age of the Son, the age of Grace and Faith. The faithful in this age—the age of St. Paul—were the Sons of God.

The third age (which Joachim predicted was to begin in 1260) would be the age of the Holy Spirit, the age of Love and Liberty. In this, the age of St. John, the faithful would be the Friends of God. The entire hierarchy would be effaced and their place taken by new spiritual teachers; the sacraments would be withdrawn; the Law and the Gospel of the two previous ages would give place to Contemplation—to 'a monachism wholly directed towards ecstasy, more Oriental than Benedictine'.

This scheme, with its emphasis on the Spirit, the gospel of Love, the appeal to the Johannine writings, and the final triumph of universal celibacy, follows the pattern and teaching with which we are by now familiar enough; and it is hardly surprising that the Church, after its initial toleration, persecuted the Joachists who had taken their master's ideas to their logical conclusion and added that forgiveness of sins could not be obtained by priestly absolution, that baptism was not essential to salvation and that ordination was less important than holiness of life. As the predicted hour of transition from the second to the third age grew uncomfortably near, the Papacy, in 1255, had the *Introduction to the Eternal Gospel* publicly burnt.

But more important than the later persecution was the original approval which demonstrates beyond cavil the thinness (indeed the practical invisibility) of the line between heresy and orthodoxy within the Church. Not only did Joachim continue to be revered and the Dominicans and Franciscans considered as the spiritual monks heralding the Third Age, but Dante, who was one of his followers, placed Joachim in Paradise; and it is possible that the *Divine Comedy* itself, properly understood, is the classic Joachist apologia.[1]

[1] See Gertrude Leigh's *New Light on the Youth of Dante* (1929) and *The Passing of Beatrice: A Study in the Heterodoxy of Dante* (1932).

Chapter XI

THE NATURE OF THE CHURCH

1. The Church and the World

The apocalyptic expectations of the Joachists were finally disappointed by the arrival of the year 1261 and the discovery that the Church and the world both continued to function very much as before. But the relationship between the Church and the world, even when not sharpened by the anticipation of the imminent gathering of the one and end of the other, is an enduring problem, from the beginning of Christianity until to-day, nor has there ever been wanting a school of thought which considers that Constantine's adoption of the Faith as the official religion of the Empire signalized the defeat rather than the triumph of the Gospel. In so far as this tension was a major factor in the Cathar movement, it may be said that the problems presented by the medieval heresy are timeless.

The continuing tension is heightened by the fact that the Christianity of the Gospels is incontrovertibly eschatological. 'The New Testament perspective is not that of an indefinite historical development, nor of a gradually expanding Christian mission, nor of a progressive realization in history of the Kingdom of God. The Christ is represented as having said: "My kingdom is not of this world." The Kingdom, the perfect reign or rule of God over His own people, was about to come. The mighty works of the Messiah, His death and resurrection, His exaltation to the right hand of God and the outpouring of the Holy Spirit, His imminent return in glory—

159

these events, which are already in motion, signify the end of the present age. The mission of the Church is to tell all who have ears to hear—as many as possible as rapidly as possible —that these final things are already happening.'[1]

In the early centuries, the mutual exclusiveness of the Church and the world was, by the circumstance of persecution, seen beyond doubt. Between the Divine Society and secular society there was a great gulf fixed; the Kingdom of God stood patently over against the kingdom of Mammon. 'The early Christians avoided contact with the State, abstained from the responsibilities of office and were even reluctant to serve in the army. Cherishing their citizenship of a kingdom not of this world, they despaired of an Empire which seemed too powerful to be resisted and too corrupt to be converted.'[2]

Constantine changed all that. With the adoption of Christianity as the official religion of the Empire, a new situation arose. The State—the expression or embodiment of 'the world'—was 'Christian', a phenomenon which had been neither envisaged nor prepared for. The 'Christian State' thus thrust upon a surprised Church was, in fact, essentially a contradiction in terms; but the existing situation had to be accepted. There was no time to work out the implications— nor have they been satisfactorily worked out to this day. 'So far as political ideas were concerned, those of the Fathers were for the most part those of Cicero and Seneca'[3]—that is to say, fundamentally pagan.

We are not concerned with the intricate and interminable argument about the Church-State relationship further than to point out that it involves a profound difference of opinion about the true nature of Christianity and is thus relevant to the subject of heresy. The usual and accepted view that 'while there is what is called a Church and State conflict throughout

---

[1] A. R. Vidler: *The Orb and the Cross* (1945).

[2] Acton: *History of Freedom* (1907).

[3] G. H. Sabine: *History of Political Theory* (1938.)

the Middle Ages, it was a conflict not between two separate
societies, but in one society between two bodies of officials,
the temporal and the spiritual, or the secular and the sacred'[1]
because 'churchmanship was co-extensive with citizenship'[2]
does not contain the whole truth. It was, in fact, precisely this
simplification which gave such force to the heretics who by
their very protest as false 'mystery religions' succeeded in
reminding the Church of its true nature and forcing it implicitly to admit that Christianity was as much a true apocalyptic mystery religion in the thirteenth as in the first century.

The force of this particular question can be the better
appreciated to-day, since in many great modern states (including our own) the wheel has turned full circle. As in the pre-
Constantine era, Christians are (as in England) a tolerated or
(as in Russia) a persecuted minority in a society which is in
fact or in name pagan and a state which acts on non-Chris-
tian or on anti-Christian assumptions. It is thus becoming
clear, even to the most unconcerned, that the Constantinian
compromise and its various interpretations in the thought of
the West through the centuries is, to say the least, unsatisfactory. Despite the fact that, in practice, the Church of
England acts as little more than a department of the Civil
Service, giving ethical sanction to the prevailing State poli-
cies, it is, of course, still possible to be a Christian within the
context of Anglicanism, though certain individual consci-
ences have, within recent memory, been troubled by the
implications of Ranyard West's neat epitome: 'A German
was as secure against death from a Quaker in 1944 as in
1934; not so from a member of the Church of England.'[3]

The difference between the Church's attitude in the contemporary situation and that in medieval times is that to-day
it merely allows instead of actively encouraging persecution
by the State, Yet, in relation to the medieval heresy—especi-

[1] Vidler: op. cit.
[2] J. N. Figgis: *Churches in the Modern State* (1914).
[3] Ranyard West: *Psychology and World Order* (1945).

ally as regards its life-denying proclivities in theory and practice—it is an open question whether, in fact (though not, of course, in theory) the crime of the Cathars in the eyes of the Church was not so much that they were anti-Christian as that they were anti-social.

Certainly the Cathars (like the Quakers) considered that the Church had made a fatal accommodation with the world; and had even reduced the sacraments to an element of that accommodation (somewhat in the manner that the Anglican Restoration settlement made a man's reception of Holy Communion a *sine qua non* of his appointment as a Justice of the Peace).

On the other hand, it is important to emphasize that, however decisively the medieval Church might act on behalf of the State, it never for one moment allowed it to be thought— as many 'modern churchmen' appear to think—that the distinguishing mark of Christianity lies in its ethical precepts.[1]

But if social morality is not the distinguishing mark of Christianity, neither is individual mystical experience. This may be made clearer by the following teaching of one of Rufus's contemporaries.

God, so this mystic avers, is the Sole-Existent and the Ultimate Cause of all being, transcendent yet immanent, the Eternal Will manifested in action throughout the universe. He is a living, personal God, perfect Goodness and Beauty, the only Object of real love. Yet He desires to enter into relationship with His creatures and makes it possible for them to

---

[1] Lest this should appear strange to those who consider that 'the Sermon on the Mount' *is* Christianity, it may be mentioned that in Christ's ethical maxims (merely as moral imperatives divorced from His Unique Personality and His Redemptive Act) there is nothing original. Those who wish a simple reference for this may find it in the appendix to C. S. Lewis's *The Abolition of Man* (1944) where he gives illustrations from the Natural Law, including the Analect of Confucius: 'Never do to others what you would not like them to do to you' and the Ancient Egyptian 'Confession of the Righteous Soul': 'I have given bread to the hungry, water to the thirsty, clothes to the naked, a ferry boat to the boatless'—precepts which are frequently, but erroneously, regarded as the essence of specifically Christian behaviour.

approach Him through prayer and contemplation and the mystic knowledge which goes beyond the senses and leads to 'union' with Him. Those to whom He reveals Himself are His Friends—the saints to whom is given the knowledge of the mysteries of God.

The path by which the soul (which belongs to the Divine world and is made in the Divine image) travels to the presence of God begins with repentance and conversion, which leads it to acknowledge humbly its creatureliness before the Creator. It turns to God with a faith which is not only outward confession but a desire for a purification of the heart from all but God. This is accomplished by confession and renunciation, so that it may be freed from the ties of this world. Eventually knowledge of God, through the intercourse of prayer, means that He is loved and His servant, now become His lover, lives a life dominated by the Spirit.[1]

At first sight this might seem orthodox Christian ascetical mysticism.[2] In point of fact it is Mohammedanism, the teaching of the famous Sufi mystic Al-Ghazali, who was born in 1058 and died in 1111.

The key to Christianity is to be found neither in general ethical correctness nor in individual experience of God by way of self-abnegation and ecstasy. Moral behaviour and mystical experience may—and indeed often do—remain quite unchristian even when decorated with a Christian terminology and practised within a Christian Church in a 'Christian State'. Neither is the resolution of the conflict between the Kingdom and the world achieved by establishing a local and temporal division in the form of a sect and calling it the 'True Church' even when this practice may appear to have some

[1] Cf. M. Smith: *Al-Ghazali the Mystic* (1944).

[2] It may be worth reminding the reader that Evelyn Underhill, writing in 1927, many years after the publication of her famous book on *Mysticism*, admitted: 'Until about five years ago I had never had *any* personal experience of our Lord. I didn't know what it meant. I was a convinced theocentric and thought most Christocentric practice sentimental and superstitious' (*Letters*: 1943). It is probable that much 'Christian' mysticism seldom deserves the adjective.

logical justification as a return to 'primitive simplicity'. Nor, certainly, is it to be found at the other extreme in the neat theory that Church and State are the same community seen in two different aspects.

The answer to the problem lies in the sacraments, which are at the same time degrees of initiation into the 'mystery' of Christianity and the means by which the inescapable duality of existence is saved from Dualism and related to unity.

2. Sacramentalism

All the parties in the medieval struggle were aware of the cardinal importance of sacramentalism. What emerged to survive as the dominating factor of subsequent history was the Church's uncompromising definition of the sacrament of the Eucharist; while, in the heresy, what the Cathars denied was the existing sacraments and what they affirmed was their own new sacrament of the Consolamentum.

The reason for this circumstance, I would suggest, was that both sides were prepared to face honestly the duality patent in the world, not only the duality of good and evil, and body and spirit, but that manifest in all natural laws and phenomena. The Gnostic explanation in terms of Dualism had, besides its stark and attractive simplicity, some empirical justification. Everyone could see that, as an explanation, it did explain; and the only real counter to postulating Dualism behind duality was to discover the factor which reduced it to unity. And this factor is sacramentalism.

The present Bishop of London—though his argument is concerned more particularly with the relation between grace and the sacraments—presents this aspect clearly enough: 'This (the Incarnation) was the supreme Sacrament, for in it the Creator took part of His universe, the human flesh and blood derived from Mary, to convey His gifts to men. Looking upon the universe as it is revealed in this example, we are able to perceive in it as a whole a vast sacrament of God's love. His mercy is over all His works and the natural world is a garment that reveals even while it conceals the form of its Creator. Obviously there are some parts and elements of this universe which are more fitted to reveal Him than others. Of these our Saviour used the most easily adaptable to continue the method of the Incarnation after His own visible presence was withdrawn from earth. To explain His relation to the Bread and the Wine, we need to remember that He called them His Body and His Blood, and that we ourselves are quite familiar with the relation between invisible personalities and the outward bodies that give them the opportunity of self-expression and of communication with others. It is true that the bread is inanimate while our bodies are animate. But we may reasonably take the Lord's relation to the sacramental Bread as equivalent to that between soul and body. And we shall be saved from all spatial crudities and helped to remember that the Presence is there as "in a sign rather than as in a vessel" if we remember that we really do not know with regard even to ourselves whether our souls are in our bodies or our bodies in our souls.'[1]

With the particulars of sacramental discussion or with theories of their mode of operation, we are not concerned. They, like the full Church-State argument, are outside this thesis. But the general relevance is clear. The sacraments are the continuing assertion and operation of the principle of unity, of Divine-human, of spirit-matter. The Word was made Flesh; the Bread is the Body; the Man Jesus is Very God; the Death is the Life. And these are not intellectual propositions for debate, but events manifest daily in a certain context and in a particular way.

> And still at certain times the steps are trod
> And still at certain times the words are said;
> Thou dost present Thyself to be our Bread,
> And we are nourished with the Body of God.[2]

[1] J. W. C. Wand: *The Development of Sacramentalism* (1928).
[2] W. R. Childe: *Hoc est Corpus Meum.*

To dispute about the exact nature of the sacramental synthesis is sooner or later to become obsessed with an analytical problem which may lure the logician into Dualism. To quote the Bishop of London again : 'At present there is a good deal of dissatisfaction in more than one sphere of thought with the category of substance. Some theologians allege, for instance, that it has led to an impasse in the field of Christology. If they begin with two distinct substances, one of Divinity and the other of humanity, they find it impossible to demonstrate logically how both can be united in the one Person of Christ. This has induced them to try another road along the line of "value" judgements, showing that the one Christ has the values of both God and man. This is parallel with an attempt to appreciate the sacraments in accordance with their psychological values.'[1]

Thus we can understand in part the wisdom of the Catholic Church, especially in the medieval contest, in discouraging general speculation about the nature of the mystery, but insisting on unquestioning devotion to the Blessed Sacrament, which was for all unreasoning and to many unreasonable. And if enemies contend that such uncritical extravagances may lead to the sin of idolatry, it may be retorted that 'idolatry' in that particular context is still nearer the truth and more patient of conversion to it than is the alternative. The 'faith' behind 'honest doubt' is apt to be something other than humble simplicity.

There is another sense in which the sacramental system corresponded with the situation which lay at the core of the conflict. The two Dominical sacraments, Baptism and Holy Communion, were explicitly initiations into the death of the Divine Victim.

No description of the meaning of Baptism as an initiatory rite could be clearer than St. Paul's : 'Know ye not that so many of us as were baptized into Jesus Christ were baptized into His Death? Therefore we are buried with Him by bap-

[1] Wand, op. cit.

tism into death; that like as Christ was raised up from the dead by the glory of the Father, even so we also should walk in newness of life. For if we have been planted together in the likeness of His Death, we shall be also in the likeness of His Resurrection.'

Baptism, however, is the initiation only, not the completion. The powers of evil still seek to impede progress in the newness of life and when they succeed the initiate must have recourse to that sacrament which is the extension of Baptism —Penance. By means of absolution the Christian is restored to the state given him at his baptism and it is only in this state—dead to sin—that he can continue his participation in the redeeming Death by feeding in Holy Communion upon the Sacred Body and Blood of the Divine Victim.[1] For to partake of the Meal in sin is to eat and drink to his own damnation.

The sacraments of confirmation and orders were grades of approach to the central mystery—confirmation both 'sealing' the initiate and giving him the right to participate in Communion and the priesthood the right to consecrate and absolve.

3. Christianity a Mystery Religion

Seen in this perspective, the relationship of the Church and the world becomes clearer. Christianity becomes fundamentally a mystery religion, that is to say, the religion of an initiate. The Church consists of those who are, or are about to be, initiated into the one and only Sacrificial Death which can alone ensure eternal life. Since this Death was for the whole world, the terms of admission to the mystery are—in glaring contradiction to other mystery religions—simple and unsecret. Unfortunately they have also become so conventional that the generality of men confuse what should be the

---

[1] 'Jesus said unto them: Verily, verily I say unto you: Except ye eat the flesh of the Son of Man and drink His blood, ye have no life in you. Whoso eateth my flesh and drinketh my blood hath eternal life and I will raise him up at the last day.'

consequence but what still remains secondary—right conduct in the world—with the purpose of initiation—which is supernatural salvation. Further, they use as their criterion of 'right' the values of the world and not of the Kingdom. It is quite true that Jesus said: 'Not every one that saith unto me "Lord! Lord!" shall enter the Kingdom of Heaven, but he that doeth the will of my Father which is in Heaven,' but this is not a general ethical precept which can be quoted against the Church by 'good men' outside it, for the simple reason, that no one but an initiate *can* know what the will of the Father is. In the most narrow and uncompromising sense, the Church remains necessary for salvation. Nor, though the terms of admission to the mystery are simple enough, is the mystery itself simple, even on the plane of conduct. St. Paul's assertion that *agape* is greater than *gnosis* is by no means an anticipation of the pleasing admonition: 'Be good, sweet maid, and let who will be clever.'

The teaching of the Church as far as the individual is concerned remains eschatological. The end of the world may not be in sight, but the earthly end of each individual undoubtedly is. Everyman has to meet Death. But the Christian initiate is, by his initiation, assured of the overcoming of Death and, with that assurance, his main concern is with eternity instead of with time.

The world is the arena of his combat for salvation; and the State the local form of organization of that part of the world in which he happens to find himself. Theoretically, the State is a neutral abstraction; it may be 'Christian'; it may be tolerant of Christianity; it may be hostile and persecuting. But, essentially, it is irrelevant except in so far as it affects the individual temperament of the Christian—that is to say, for some natures it is easier to walk in the Way in a persecuting than in a tolerant State.

The tension that arises when the Church, by reason of indolent or evil persons in high places within it, compromises with the State is really an issue of minor importance, though

168

in practice it looms so large at times that it is mistaken for an essential; and argument—like that which led to the Albigensian heresy or the Protestant schism—starts wrongly from it as a premiss. But schism is at once seen as the gravest of sins, once the nature of the Sacramental Mystery is grasped. For 'although in the visible Church the evil be ever mingled with the good, and sometimes the evil has chief authority in the ministration of the Word and the Sacraments, yet forasmuch as they do not the same in their own name but in Christ's and do minister by His commission and authority, we may use their ministry'.[1]

The reluctance still found in certain quarters to concede that Christianity is a mystery religion is due partly to this (for schismatics usually understand quite clearly the consequences of admitting it) and partly to the genuine fear that the phrase will be interpreted as meaning that it is merely a syncretistic derivation from pagan 'mysteries' and not Revealed Truth. But such fear is surely groundless when it is understood that those other 'mysteries' were human attempts to deal with the same problems of the universe as those to which the Incarnation supplied the answer; and that their solution naturally followed similar lines, so that the very ambiguities with which this essay has been concerned are only comprehensible in the theological context which, at first sight, seems far removed from the arrow in the New Forest and the sword in Canterbury Cathedral.

[1] Book of Common Prayer: Article XXVI,

Chapter XII

AGAPE AND EROS: A NOTE

The approach to religion by way of the meaning of love and the employment of the distinguishing terms Agape and Eros has been increasingly occupying recent thought. Within the last ten years three important books have appeared, *Agape and Eros* by Anders Nygren, which was available in full in English in 1938; *Passion and Society* by Denis de Rougemont, which appeared in translation in 1940; and *The Mind and Heart of Love*, by the English Jesuit, Martin D'Arcy, published in 1945.

Dr. Nygren's thesis is that Agape, Christian love, and Eros, Plato's 'Heavenly Love' belong to two different spiritual worlds, that 'they do not stand for the same thing in their respective contexts nor can they under any circumstances be treated as synonyms'—an injunction doubly difficult to observe since, in the first place 'for much more than a thousand years the two ideas of love have been blended together and confused in all parts of Christendom' and, in the second, that in our modern languages the one word 'Love' does duty for both the Greek words. He considers that 'the meeting of Agape and Eros was Christianity's hour of destiny', sees in the ideas associated with them, two opposite attitudes to life, two different answers to the fundamental question of man.

As he analyses it, Agape is God's way to man, Eros, man's way to God; thus Eros is man's effort to ascend, but Agape the Divine descent. 'Eros is primarily human love and God is the object of Eros; Agape is primarily God's own love, for

God is Agape. Eros, when it is applied to God, is a love fashioned after the pattern of human love; Agape, when it appears in man, is a love which takes its form from God's own love. Eros recognizes value in its object and therefore loves it; Agape loves and creates value in its object.'

The author's account of European thought in terms of Agape and Eros thus defined is, granting his premise, brilliant and, even denying it, valuable and suggestive. He sees Eros in Gnosticism, a synthesis of Eros and Agape in Origen (who equates Agape with 'Heavenly Eros') and Augustine; and the re-emergence of Eros in the Pseudo-Dionysius (who considers Eros 'more Divine' than Agape).

M. de Rougemont follows the differentiation between Agape and Eros in theory, though in practice he tends to modify and alter it. He is concerned with the romantic obsession with passionate love, the love that is eternally unfulfilled and brings in its train suffering, separation and death, the love which finds its 'myth' for the West in the story of Tristan and Iseult. He traces its origin to the 'courtly' love of the twelfth century, with its first European expression in the lyricism of the Troubadours, at the back of which lies, as he sees, the inheritance of Gnostic dualism. The antithesis of this love is the Christian ideal of marriage.

'The cultivation of passionate love began', he writes, 'in Europe as a reaction to Christianity (and in particular to its doctrine of marriage) by people whose spirit, whether naturally or by inheritance, was still pagan. . . .

'Christian love—which is Agape—is the expression of being. And it is Eros, passionate love, pagan love, that spread through the European world the poison of an idealistic askesis—all that Nietzsche unjustly lays at the door of Christianity. And it is Eros, not Agape, that glorified our death instinct and sought to "idealize it". . . . The god Eros is the slave of death because he wishes to elevate life above our finite and limited creature state. Hence the same impulse that leads us to adore life thrusts us into its negation. There lies

the profound woe and despair characterizing Eros, his in-
expressible bondage; and in making this bondage evident
Agape has delivered Eros from it. Agape is aware that our
terrestrial and temporal life is unworthy of adoration and
even of being killed, but that it can be accepted in obedience
to the Eternal.'

Much of Father D'Arcy's book is occupied with an examination and criticism of the theses of Nygren and de Rougemont. In the course of his penetrating summary, he writes
'De Rougemont thinks of Eros as unrestrained and passionate, hedonistic and to that extent selfish, but also bent on
self-destruction and fusion of its identity with the dark god-
head. To Nygren it is the rational man, the natural man of
the Scriptures, who relies upon himself and is fundamentally
egocentric, who is moved by Eros. Eros belongs to the Greek
way of life . . . (and) . . . is equivalent to self-love. The Christian love, which Nygren calls Agape, does not negotiate with
this self-love at all; it discards it utterly. God does everything; He is Agape and freely, without any regards for the
deserts of human beings, He initiates a corresponding Agape
in them. . . .

'Whereas, then, de Rougemont considers Eros to be unrestrained and passionate, and apparently more inclined to
self-effacement than to self-regard, Nygren defines it as an
Hellenic ideal, as intellectual, self-complacent and possessive,
as, in short, irretrievably egocentric. Agape, on the other
hand, in Nygren's view is so theocentric as to leave nothing
human in it, while de Rougemont sees in it something which
irradiates reason and everything human. By God's love, as
the latter says, "every human relationship has been given a
new *direction* in being given a new *meaning*". It is strange
that two such penetrating observers should come to such
strikingly different conclusions. On one point, however, they
concur—Eros is somehow connected with the growth of Neo-
Platonism. . . . One thinks that the dark passion took philosophical shape when in its journey from the East it encoun-

tered Greek thought; the other is convinced that the egocentric philosophy of Greece soared up into a mystical religion when it encountered the mystery religions of the East.
The only difference here is one of stress; the result is the same,
except that de Rougemont limits the enemies of Agape to
Gnosticism, while Nygren includes the whole of Hellenic
philosophy and religion.'

By countering the overstress on both sides, Father D'Arcy
makes them yield a complete anatomy of the nature of love,
whose two aspects are necessary complements in every human
being. 'Nygren, then, presents us with self-love and its most
powerful instrument, the human reason; de Rougemont presents us with a romantic and ecstatic love, which is either
irrational or ill at ease at the superior claims upon it of
reason. One love takes and possesses; the other love likes to
be beside itself and give. One is masculine, the other feminine.
The two are necessary for one another and together they tell
us what we are and whither we are going. To neglect either
is to court death.'

To the self-regarding, masculine, rational, dominating
aspect of love, Father D'Arcy gives the name *animus*; to the
self-immolating, feminine, 'spiritual', desiring-to-be-domin-
ated aspect, *anima*; and from this postulate works out at
some length and with immense erudition its theological and
philosophical, its metaphysical and psychological implications. He uses it as a key to the understanding of the relationships of man with God, of man with the universe, of man with
individuals and of man with society. 'The two kinds of love,
which we distinguished as "taking" and "giving", masculine
and feminine, centripetal and centrifugal, which are contained in Eros and Agape and expressed in part by *animus*
and *anima* are seen in a new distinction of nature and person,
or better still of essence and existence.' The thesis, however,
is both too closely-knit and too complex for any abstract to
do it justice and I can only refer readers to the book itself
which for a full understanding must be studied in full.

For the purposes of my own approach to Agape and Eros (which was formulated before the publication of *The Mind and Heart of Love*) the important clue is Father D'Arcy's demonstration of what may be termed the bisexual nature of individual love. 'The splitting up into different genders', he says, 'marks clearly the contrast between the two loves and desires. It does not matter whether in any particular species the male or the female be dominant. In the brute creation the two desires or impulses or instincts (the name does not matter in this regard) are more obvious because they approach our own experience and can therefore more easily be judged. The male is dominant, self-assertive and violent; the female is responsive to his pleasures, but looks instinctively beyond its mate to offspring and the continuation of the species.'

The sexual distinction, however, is valid in more than a symbolic sense. It reinforces the conclusion of psychologists that there is no such thing as a 'normal' male or 'normal' female, but that everyone, in varying proportions, partakes of the nature of both sexes; and thus it leads back to the categories of 'biological' and 'Uranian' love which I have used earlier, and which, though explicit in Plato, are virtually ignored by the three writers we have been discussing. This ignoring results in certain confusions in their categories.

Nygren's thesis has been criticized from various angles, but the major theological objection to it is that he so overstresses the transcendence of God that it becomes virtually impossible for man to love Him. As the Rev. E. L. Mascall puts it: 'In the course of his historical study, Nygren most scrupulously and charitably defends the great Catholic saints from practically all the charges that Protestantism has ever brought against them; there is only one fault of which he cannot acquit them, that of trying to love God.'[1] But it might be argued that even this false emphasis springs from his refusal to face what Plato's 'Heavenly Eros' in fact is. When, for example, he points to the fundamental quality of Agape as

[1] E. L. Mascall: *He Who Is* (1943).

that 'it loves and creates value in its object', it might be answered that this precisely is the distinguishing mark of the Platonic Eros where 'the God is in the Lover, not in the Beloved'. And no one, reading *Agape and Eros* without having first read the *Symposium* and the *Phaedrus* would be likely to gather from Nygren's summary of their teaching that Heavenly Eros is 'felt only for males'.

A similar confusion vitiates the whole of de Rougemont's argument. When he describes 'the poison of an idealistic *askesis*' as the work of Eros, he is allowing it to be assumed that Eros is love between the sexes, which, on Plato's definition, it cannot possibly be. But the homosexual nature of Eros, and nothing else, is the reason why it *must* be unindulged. Its death is, *ipso facto*, the condition of its life. But this quality of necessary unfulfilment is obviously not applicable to love between the sexes. The deliberate abstention from the fulfilment of a natural biological love is something totally different in kind from the ascetic discipline which prevents 'Platonic love' becoming an indulged perversion. The *askesis* of which de Rougemont complains is a poison only when the *askesis* proper to homosexual love becomes transferred to and made a mark of value in heterosexual love. Then, indeed, it does become, as de Rougemont insists, an expression of 'death' instead of 'life'.

My own suggestion that Agape is crucified and resurrected Eros has at least the advantage of allowing for the true nature of Eros and of being consistent with historical manifestations and theological beliefs.

Once the dual nature of human love is faced, its apparently contradictory manifestations are seen as complementary, each with its own law. In its 'normal' aspect, where each sex expresses the emotions and desires proper to itself, the male his masculinity, the female her femininity, the law is not of abstention but of fulfilment, and the only *askesis* imposed is that of the sacrament of marriage. The renunciation demanded is the putting away of others 'as long as ye both do live'—a binding vow because the physical act brings into the world not only a new body but a new soul to whom the contracting parties have a responsibility which promiscuity makes it impossible to honour.

But in the other love, the *askesis*, as regards physical expression, is absolute. The creativity of this love is in the realm of the spirit, whose sensitivity is sharpened by denial on the plane of matter. Here—and probably here alone[1]— love in and of the spirit is understood; it is the way of artists and mystics, irrespective of creed; and, within the Christian context, the way of the lovers of God.

It may clarify this distinction to quote from M. Etienne Gilson's *The Mystical Theology of St. Bernard* where, in a long appendix on 'St. Bernard and Courtly Love' he is at pains to rebut the suggestion that Bernard's 'mystical love' and the 'courtly love' of the Troubadours have similarities which suggest a mutual indebtedness. He writes: 'Human love is never fully realized save in that union of man and woman which makes them one flesh. Man is a carnal being; therefore the union of two human beings, if it is to be complete, cannot be limited to a union of thought or affection, or even, to adopt the language of André-le-Chapelain, of contemplation, but must be a union of the whole being. No other relation of human being to human being is to be compared with that, not even that of parents to children. . . .

'The mystic can have no thought of union with God by way of his body (albeit this body is hereafter to participate in beatitude) for God is Spirit; but in the order at least of spiritual life which is his, he will never conceive a union of love which is not, in its own way, total. . . . In short, pure courtly love is defined by exclusion of that precisely which constitutes the pure love of the mystics; the real union of

---

[1] I do not, of course, mean to imply that spiritual love is impossible between man and woman, but that the temporary circumstances which, by denying bodily fulfilment, call it into existence make it approximate to the permanent nature of homosexual love—as in the case of Dante and Beatrice.

lover and beloved. . . . The mystic and the courtly poet, although both renounce, the one all and the other certain of the joys of the body the better to assure the spiritual purity of their love, move none the less in opposite directions; for the mystic, putting the problem of love between his spirit and the Spirit, can resolve it integrally while sacrificing nothing of the exigencies of love; he aspires therefore to the delights of the Divine Union and there it is that love finds its purity. The courtly poet, putting the love between two beings of flesh, can conceive of purity only in the exclusion of all real union between those beings; so that the purity of courtly love keeps the lovers apart, while that of mystical love unites them.'

Here Gilson makes the same mistake as de Rougemont. Whether or not it is in fact true that 'human love is never fully realized save in that union of man and woman which makes them one flesh', it is incontrovertible that Plato did not think so; and that what Gilson regards as the highest manifestation of love, Plato dismisses as unworthy of consideration in the debate on the nature of Eros. Since the courtly poets were taking for granted Plato's premises, it is pointless—to use no harsher word—to attack them on the assumption that they were talking about its opposite. It is true that 'putting the problem of love between two beings of flesh and blood' they conceived of purity 'only in the exclusion of all real union between those beings', but that was a necessity of the particular relationship, not an eccentric asceticism. And it is also true that, having to resolve the problem on the plane of spirit, they found their union in a way which is closely analagous to the mystic's love of God— a problem between spirit and spirit to be resolved 'while sacrificing nothing of the exigencies of love'.

Even if it be admitted that the solution in practice is often partial and unsatisfactory and that, even at its best, it always remains a love of creatures (though, since there is neither possession nor gratification, a genuinely unselfish love) it is still a preparation for the true mystic love of God, in that, even while it is earth-bound in its object, it instinctively understands the meaning of Divine love as manifested in the Christian revelation. The crucifixion of Eros results in the Agape which *is* the condition of union; and through that Agape the heart is also opened to receive the outpouring of the very love of God Himself.

INDEX

Abraham, 9, 62
Adam, Karl, 2
Agape, 78, 79, 168, Chapter xii
   passim
Ahriman, 25, 28, 29, 38, 42, 44,
   45, 46, 101
Akhnaton, 59, 60, 61, 65
Albigenses, 8, 16, 48–52, 124, 139,
   140 (*see also* Cathars)
Aleion, 24
Alexander the Great, 10, 36, 63,
   66, 83, 116
Alexandria, 13, 14
Al-Ghazali, 163
Anselm, 118, 120, 124
Antiochus IV, 63
Apuleius, 27
Arnold, Dr., 91
Arthurian cycle, 54–57
Asceticism, 102, 103, 175, 176
Astrology, 36, 44, 66 (*see also*
   Stars)
Astarte, 25, 62, 68, 69
Attis, 24
Augustine of Canterbury, St., 95
Augustine of Hippo, St., 12, 14,
   34, 41, 43, 80, 86

Baal, 25, 30, 59, 62
Babylon, 9, 15, 25, 31, 33, 36, 66
Baptism, 148, 150, 166, 167
Becket, Thomas, 1, 7, 17, 35, 69,
   70, 95, 103–105, chapter vii
   passim
Bernard of Clairvaux, St., 69, 82,
   122, 135, 142, 151, 176
Bernart of Ventadorn, 121
Bishop, Functions of, 102
Bledri, 54, 115
Bleheris, 54

Blondel, 121
Bossuet, 139, 140, 141
Bulgars, 16, 48
Bull, the, 20, 21, 23, 24, 37, 44, 45,
   56, 112

Cadivor, 54, 113
Cæsar, Julius, 52, 53, 80
Canterbury, 120, 128, 169
Carthage, 10
Cathars, 16, 49, 96, 103, chapter ix
   passim, 159, 162
Celibacy, clerical, 154, 155
Chaldaeans, 9, 10, 30, 35
Chalcedon, Council of, 13
'Chariot', the, 33
Chivalry, 83, 84, 91, 109, 116
Christmas Day, 40, 73
Church and State, 159 *et seq*, 165,
   168
Chyndonax, the Arch-Druid, 53
Circumcision, 61
Colobium, 111
'Consolamentum', the, 49, 126,
   127, 146, 147, 164
Constantine the Great, 13, 156,
   159, 160
Constantius Sylvanus, 16
Cornwall, 52
Creed,
   the Athanasian, 152
   the Nicene, 13, 74

Dance, the Ring, 96 *et seq.*
Dante, 15, 158
d'Arcy, Martin, S.J., 170 *et seq.*
Demant, V. A., 2, 4
Demiurge, the, 42, 49, 100
de Rougemont, Denis, 84, 170 *et
   seq.*

Destiny, 37, 115
'Devil', the, 100, 104–106, 101, 119, 125, 135, 154
Diana, 92
Diocletian, 12
Dionysius the Areopagite, 14, 102
'Divine Victim', the, 1, 7, 17, 19, 20, 104, 106, 111, 118, 120, 134, 153, 154, 167
Dragon, the, 25, 30, 31, 35, 118
Druidism, 52, 53, 92
Dualism, 141, 164, 166

Eleanor of Aquitaine, 121
Eliot, T. S., 2, 3
Endura, the, 127, 150, 151
Epiphanius, 42
Eros, 8, 78, 79, 85, chapter xii passim
Exile, the Jewish, 61, 65, 66
Exodus, the Jewish, 61
Ezekiel, 33

Faber, G. S., 139–142
Fire as first principle, 37
Flambard, Ranulf, 104, 115
Four, the number, 32–35, 130, 131
Four-faced Father, 46
Francis of Assisi, St., 156
Friars, 155, 156

Gaskell, G. A., 74
Gerizim, Mount, 62, 63, 64, 70
Giants, the Somerset, 57
Gilson, Etienne, 176, 177
Gnosis, 39, 40, 41, 43, 46, 102, 168
Gnosticism, 12, 13, 15, 41, 43, 45, 50, 56, 72, 96, 100, 135, 144, 151
Golden Bough, The, 8, 19
Grail, the, 54, 55, 56, 57, 93, 104, 115
Greece, 36, 52

Harnack, Adolf von, 12
Helias of Maine, 113, 114, 121
Helios, 37, 71 (see also Sun)
Heliopolis, 23
Hellenism, 13, 37
Henry II, 105, 120, 121, 122, 123, 124, 125

Heraclitus of Ephesus, 38
Hocart, A. M., 24
Honey as lustral agent, 56
Hooke, S. H., 24
Horus, 25

Immaculate Conception, the, 69, 135
Incense, 33, 68
Initiation, rites of, 26, 27, 93
Initiation, grades of:
  Christian, 167
  Cathar, 49, 50, 149
  Manichean, 48
  Gnostic, 43
  Mithraic, 44, 55
  Philonic, 39
Isaiah, 9, 30, 31, 66, 67, 68
Ishtar, 22, 25
Isis, 23, 25, 60, 62
Innocent III, 142, 152

Jehovah, 25, 42, 61, 64, 100
Jerusalem, 11, 59, 62, 64, 65, 66, 68, 134
Jesus Christ, 9, 11, 45, 46, 47, 48, 63, 64, 70, 71, 72, 74, 85, 97, 100, 111, 152, 153, 164, 165, 167
Joachim of Floris, 157, 158
St. John:
  Acts of, 86, 97, 112
  Apocalypse of, 8, 30, 31, 50, 51, 157
  Apocryphal literature concerning, 85
  Epistle of, 47, 99
  Gospel of, 8, 34, 40, 71, 75, 145
  'Prologue' to, 39, 40, 43, 49, 126, 147, 156
John of Salisbury, 116, 124, 131
Joseph of Arimathea, 52
Julian the Apostate, 13, 116
Justinus, 52

King, the, 23, 24 (see also Divine Victim)
Kiss of Peace, the, 49, 50, 126, 127, 147
Kosti, the, 49, 50, 71, 147
Knox, W. L., 33, 68

Lazarus, the raising of, 34
Lateran Council of 1215, 124, 135, 152–155, 157
Leviathan, 30 (*see also* Dragon)
Lewis, C. S., 84, 162
Light and Dark, 47, 48, 144
Logos:
　the Christian, 39, 40, 55, 70
　the Philonic, 38, 39, 73
　the Stoic, 38
Lucca, the Holy Face of, 111, 112, 113

Mani, 46, 133
Manicheism, 8, 12, 13, 34, 46–49, 86, 102, 111, 140
Magi, the, 31
Marduk, 25, 30, 36
Mary, the Virgin, 48, 69, 70, 144, 156
Mascall, E. L., 174
Minotaur, the, 24
Mithra, 8, 10, 11, 12, 20, 21, chapter iii *passim*, 73, 134
Mithraism, 11, 13, chapter iii *passim*, 72, 73, 74, 94, 104, 151
Mithradates, 10, 12
Mithraeum, 53, 56
Moon, the, 35, 44, 53
Moses, 59, 60, 61
Murray, Margaret, 7, 95, 117

Necessity, 31, 132
New Forest, 7, 107, 108, 110, 117, 169
Nicaea:
　First Council of, 13
　Second Council of, 86, 99
Nicodemus, 111
Nile, the, 23
North, the, 132, 133
Numbers, properties of, 31
Nygren, Anders, 170 *et seq.*

Ogdoad, the, 43
Olives, Mount of, 65, 97
Ormuzd, 10, 28, 29, 37, 38, 42, 45, 46
Orpheus, 83
Osiris, 24, 60, 66, 110

Paradise, 43, 44, 71
Pattern, the Ritual, 23, 24, 25
Paul, St., 16, 85, 157, 166
Paulicianism, 16, 48, 86, 111, 140
Penance, 148, 150, 154, 167
Persia, 10, 28, 29, 30, 36
Philistines, 58
Philo, 35, 38, 39,
Phythian-Adams W . J., 55, 56
Plato, 8, 10, 76, 77, 78, 175, 177
Plutarch, 34, 41
Poitou, the Count of, 113, 121
Pompey the Great, 11, 12
Priscillianism, 16
Provence, 16, 50, 51
Pythagoras, 32, 33, 143

Rationalism, 3
Raven, the, 21, 55, 56
Read, Herbert, 3
Red, 110
Red Heifer, the, 65
Richard I, 121
Robe, the Seamless, 71
Rufus, William, 1, 7, 9, 17, 105, chapter vii *passim*, 120, 134

Sacraments:
　Christian, 148, 164–167
　Cathar, 147–150
Sacred Band, the, 83
Sargon, 63
Samaritans, 62, 65
Schism, 169
Sennacherib, 9
Set, 25
Seven:
　Heavens, 43
　Ladders, 44
　Powers, 42
　Stations, 56
Shamash, 30, 37
Shakespeare, William, 79
Silvester II, Pope, 96
Simon Magus, 63
Sol Invictus, cult of, 12, 13, 40, 156
Solomon, 9, 62, 64
Soderblom, Archbishop, 71
Spirit, the, 74, 75, 87, 145, 146, 158

INDEX

Stars, the, 31, 35, 37, 56
Stoicism, 37, 38
Sun, the, 23, 55, 60, 61, 64, 65, 66, 71, 106

Tarot, the, 33
Tammuz, 22, 24, 71
Temple, the, 64, 65, 66, 68
Tennyson, Alfred Lord, 81
Theodore of Tarsus, 92, 95
Thompson, Francis, 42
Tiamat, 25, 30, 35, 42
Tirel, Sir Walter, 108, 116, 117
Toulouse, Synod of, 17
Transubstantiation, 153, 154, 164
Troubadours, the, 8, 17, 50, 54, 84, 104, 115, 119, 121, 155
Trinity:
  the Holy, 34, 86, 143, 145, 146, 152, 157
  the Cathar, 143–146
Tyrell, George, 3

Urania, Venus, 78

Uranianism, 65, Chapter v *passim*, 116, 174–177

Vegetation offering, 21, 22
Veronica, St., 113
Vidler, A. R., 3, 160

Wand, J. W. C., 164, 165, 166
Warner, H. J., 141, 143
Weston, J. L., 54, 93
William II, *see* Rufus
William IX of Aquitaine, 113
Winchester, 119
Wisdom, 66, 67, 68
Witchcraft, 91, 92, 93, 104, 105, 151

'Young King', the, 121, 123, 125, 135

Zeno, 37
Zeus, 37, 63
Zion, Mount, 50, 62, 63, 64, 66, 68–70, 75
Zodiac, the, 36, 56
Zoroaster, 28, 46, 71